The

About the Book

Most people are attracted by the brooding majesty or pic-
turesque ruins of castles. This book provides a wealth of
detailed information about them, explaining how and why
castles were built, and how much they cost. It examines
their role not only in war, but also in peacetime when they
were the centres of estate management and local government. It sets out the development of military architecture
between the 11th and 16th centuries, and the changing
methods of siege and defence. For the visitor, the compo-
nent parts of castles, such as keeps, gate-houses, hall and
kitchens, are individually described. There is a gazetteer of
examples of castles in the British Isles, all open to the public,
and an invaluable site list denoting where good examples of
particular features may be viewed. The book is well illus-
trated with plans, drawings, photographs and maps.

About the Author

Brian Davison is an Inspector of Ancient Monuments for the
Historic Buildings and Monuments Commission for England, and has directed excavations at the sites of several
early Norman Castles, as well as at Hampton Court, Windsor
Castle and the Tower of London. An established authority
on early Norman fortifications in England, he is currently
preparing the first comprehensive survey of early castles in
Normandy. He was brought up in Northern Ireland, but now
lives with his family in Sussex.

WITHDRAWN

As well as the paperback *New Observer's* guides, there are hardback *Observers* too, covering a wide range of topics.

NATURAL HISTORY Birds Birds' Eggs Wild Animals Farm Animals Sea Fishes Butterflies Larger Moths Caterpillars Sea and Seashore Cats Trees Grasses Cacti Gardens Roses House Plants Vegetables Geology Fossils

SPORT AND LEISURE Golf Tennis Sea Fishing Music Folk Song Jazz Big Bands Sewing Furniture Architecture Churches

COLLECTING Awards and Medals Glass Pottery and Porcelain Silver Victoriana Firearms Kitchen Antiques

TRANSPORT Small Craft Canals Vintage Cars Classic Cars Manned Spaceflight Unmanned Spaceflight

TRAVEL AND HISTORY London Devon and Cornwall Cotswolds World Atlas European Costume Ancient Britain Heraldry

The New Observer's Book of

Castles

Brian K. Davison,
BA, FSA, MIFA

with 46 line drawings by
Jasper Dimond,
12 black and white illustrations
and 3 maps

Frederick Warne

FREDERICK WARNE
Penguin Books Ltd, Harmondsworth, Middlesex, England
Viking Penguin Inc., 40 West 23rd Street, New York, New York 10010, U.S.A.
Penguin Books Australia Ltd, Ringwood, Victoria, Australia
Penguin Books Canada Limited, 2801 John Street, Markham, Ontario, Canada L3R 1B4
Penguin Books (N.Z.) Ltd, 182–190 Wairau Road, Auckland 10, New Zealand

First published 1979
Reprinted 1980
Second edition 1986

Copyright © Frederick Warne & Co., 1979, 1986

Originally published as *The Observer's Book of Castles*
in small hardback format

ISBN 0 7232 3339 X

Printed and bound in Great Britain by
Butler & Tanner Ltd,
Frome and London

CONTENTS

ACKNOWLEDGEMENTS

Thanks are given to the following copyright owners and photographers for their kind permission to reproduce photographs in this book:
Musée de Condé, Chantilly, France (photograph, Photographie Giraudon), page 12: Crown Copyright Reserved, pages 13, 26, 70, 75 (pages 13 and 75 by permission of the Welsh Office, and page 70 with permission of the Controller of Her Majesty's Stationery Office): Copyright Reserved, page 20: Estate of the late Alan Sorrell, pages 23, 31, 97: The National Trust, page 87: The Phaidon Press Ltd, page 57: The Trustees of Sir John Soane's Museum, page 67.

ILLUSTRATIONS

PREFACE

I have always enjoyed looking at castles. Few buildings
are so dramatic in their appearance and so evocative in
their ruin. I hope that this book will help others to enjoy
castles and to look at them with a greater understanding
of their meaning in the landscape.

Many people have helped in the writing of this
book—though they may not always have realized it.
I owe a debt of gratitude to Martyn Jope, who first
taught me how to look at castles. Among many later
colleagues and friends I would like to single out Reg-
inald Allen Brown, Peter Curnow and Derek Renn.
I am also deeply indebted to Jasper Dimond for his
illustrations.

In a book of this sort it is not possible to acknowledge
the source of many statements. It would be wrong,
however, not to mention the published works of
Patrick Faulkner on domestic planning in castles.

Finally, I would like to thank my wife Sheila and my
three daughters Roisin, Grainne and Fionnuala, who
have shivered in the rain and fallen into overgrown
ditches more times than anyone should be asked to
endure—usually without complaint!

Brian K. Davison

I LOOKING AT CASTLES

Today the medieval castles of Britain lie about the landscape like stranded whales left high and dry by a receding tide, reminding us of an earlier and very different world. Only a few castles retain anything of their original role. Windsor has remained a royal residence throughout the nine hundred years of its history, and at Lincoln the Crown Court still sits in the bailey of the castle, where the king's officers have given judgment since 1068. For the most part, however, the castles lie in ruins, almost a part of the natural scenery.

It was quite different in the Middle Ages. Then the castles dominated the landscape. Whereas the modern citizen must look hard to find his Town Hall, the medieval centres of power and authority were plain to see. The castles dwarfed the surrounding houses of the merchants and peasants in a way that is difficult to appreciate in an age accustomed to tall buildings on every side. Some idea of the effect can be got from the coloured illustrations in French manuscripts of the time (see page 12). While we cannot be certain that every castle looked exactly like those shown—most British castles were probably more squat and sombre—the illustrations do tell us how the medieval nobles who built these castles liked to think of them.

Even now, castles are often seen as symbols of an age of romance, suggesting chivalry and glory. In reality, however, they bear witness to an age of violence, reminding us of rebellion and repression. We may enjoy exploring their remains. We should not lament their passing.

The French Castle of Saumur, from a 15th-century
manuscript: the vision...

...and the reality: the small 13th-century castle of Castell Coch in South Wales, as rebuilt in the 1870s

Castles and Historians Historians' attitudes to castles and the part they played in medieval life have varied greatly in the past—and no doubt will continue to do so in the future. This is particularly so in respect of early Norman castles. The first castles were the product of the Norman Conquest, and the Conquest has intrigued, puzzled and exasperated historians for centuries. It was the last time the British (or, in this case, the English) were defeated on their own ground by an invading army. Opinion has been divided as to how this subjugation could ever have come about, but most historians are agreed that castles played a major role. A modern historian who thinks that the Norman Conquest was, on the whole, a 'good thing' will tend to portray the castles of the new Norman king and his knights rather as the Victorians saw the colonial works of the British in Africa and India—as symbols of civilization and order. A historian who is less impressed by the Normans will portray their castles as the symbols of tyranny—built by forced labour and used to enforce an alien regime.

These opposing views of the medieval castle can be seen (and enjoyed, if you like a good fight) in the writings of J. H. Round and E. A. Freeman at the end of the last century. The furore they caused then has died down somewhat by now, but echoes can still be found in most books on castles. Differences of approach must be expected if you wish to pursue the subject in greater depth than can be done in this book.

Visiting The medieval castle was first and foremost a private house, the heavily defended residence of its lord. A considerable number still remain in private hands: these castles are usually open to the public for at least part of the year, and most will have some form of guide-book on sale to visitors.

The National Trust owns about 20 castles in England,

Wales and Northern Ireland. Details of these, with hours of opening and admission prices, are to be found in *Properties of the National Trust*, available from 36 Queen Anne's Gate, London SW1H 9AS. Details of castles owned by the National Trust for Scotland can be obtained from 5 Charlotte Square, Edinburgh EH2 4DU. Guide-books are available in most cases.

Many of the larger and more ruinous castles are in the care of the following bodies, from whom details are obtainable:

England English Heritage, 15–17 Great Marlborough St., London W1V 1AF (or at any English Heritage site).

Wales CADW, Brunel House, 2 Fitzalan Rd., Cardiff CF2 1UY.

Scotland Scottish Development Department, 3–11 Melville St., Edinburgh EH3 7QD.

Northern Ireland Department of the Environment (N. Ireland), 66 Balmoral Avenue, Belfast BT9 6NY.

Republic of Ireland Office of Public Works, 51 St Stephen's Green, Dublin 2.

How to Use this Book Many of the books in this series are concerned with recognition. There are reference books to enable you to identify any flower, bird, aircraft, etc., you may come across. This approach is hardly appropriate for medieval castles. For one thing, you don't come across all that many castles in the course of a day's outing: for another, most of those you do come across will have their own guide-book telling you all you need to know about the place—who built it, and why, who besieged it, and so on.

This book sets out to explain something about the people who built castles and why they found it necessary to do so. There is a brief outline in Chapter III of the main trends in military architecture from the 11th to the 15th centuries. Chapter IV describes the methods of attack and defence practised during the relatively brief periods when castles came under siege, while Chapter V attempts to give some idea of the pattern of life during those longer periods of peace when castles were centres of domestic life, estate management and local administration. Chapters VI and VII, together with the illustrations, should enable you to make your own guess as to when a castle was built, when it was altered, and what sort of activities went on inside it.

The Gazetteer at the end of the book lists a number of castles in Britain and Ireland open to the public. Some of these were built 'all of a piece', and demonstrate the best that the military architects of that time could achieve. Others were altered regularly over several centuries, and so demonstrate not only the changing requirements of their owners, but also developments in the art or science of fortification.

In order to avoid cluttering up the text by quoting examples of each type of tower, gate or chapel, numbers have been placed in the margins of the pages. These refer to the castles listed in the Gazetteer. Finally, the Site Lists on page 184, where the numbers similarly refer to the Gazetteer, should enable you to work out which castles to visit if you want to see a special type of keep, for example, or a particular period of building.

Further Reading If you wish to pursue the study of castles further, these books will help you:

Armitage, E. S., 1912. *The Early Norman Castles of the British Isles.* John Murray. Republished 1971 by Gregg International Publishers

Renn, D. F., 1973. *Norman Castles in Britain.* 2nd Edition. John Baker

Brown, R. A., 1976. *English Castles.* 3rd Edition. Batsford

Cruden, S., 1960. *The Scottish Castle.* Nelson

Leask, H. G., 1941. *Irish Castles and Castellated Houses.* W. Tempest

II THE KNIGHT AND HIS CASTLE

One of the results of the collapse of the Western Roman Empire in the 4th and 5th centuries under the assaults of the barbarian Huns, Franks, Saxons, Goths and Vandals, was the disappearance of a paid army distinct from the domestic retinues of the aristocracy. In the ensuing Middle Ages, armies were composed largely of groups of individuals led by those to whom in peace they owed economic or political allegiance. The aristocrat had become of necessity a professional fighter, a war leader; his private house—suitably defended—had become his fort and, in effect, part of his equipment as a warrior.

To understand how this came about it is necessary to look at Germany and France during the five centuries or so following the end of the Roman Empire. In this 'dark age' the greatest of the Frankish rulers, Charlemagne, attempted to restore something of the political and cultural order of the Roman Empire: but under the attack of a fresh wave of barbarians—this time the Vikings—his sons were forced to entrust the defence of the coastline and the rivers which led into the heart of France and Germany to the landed aristocracy of those areas. As communications broke down and the central authority waned, the rich, the powerful and the unscrupulous came to occupy positions which combined social and economic patronage with military and legal authority. A chain of command evolved which depended not on service to the state but on service to one's lord—a hierarchy of personal relationships. So was born the form of society which later historians were to call 'feudal'.

As society changed, so too did the methods of fighting. Against marauders from the sea, who could strike swiftly and unexpectedly in places far apart, the best weapon was cavalry. The basic fighting unit of the early Middle Ages was thus the heavily armed cavalryman. But the cavalryman, when dismounted, was as vulnerable as the infantryman. His horse—the most expensive part of his equipment—was even more vulnerable. Some form of protection was needed for man and horse when off duty. The fortified houses of the aristocracy gave both protection against surprise attack and a base from which mounted war bands could strike back. Thus the vital combination of knight and castle was forged.

In Anglo-Saxon England, Viking attack brought, not a breakdown in public authority but rather a strengthening of it. The army bases of the Saxon kings of the later 9th and 10th centuries were fortified towns rather than the fortified private houses of the nobility. Only during the last two or three generations before the Norman Conquest, when the Saxon defence system crumbled under the onslaught of the Danish kings Sweyn Forkbeard and Canute the Great, do the Saxon aristocracy seem to have sought security by fortifying their houses.

Beyond England, however, lay the Celtic lands of Wales, Scotland and Ireland. Here, in the absence of any developed concept of the state, society was again organized round the persons of the aristocracy. Chiefs and petty kings held court in houses fortified through the labour of their subjects according to customary law. In these centres—*llys*, *dun* or *rath*—they heard disputes and dispensed justice. Here taxes were paid and the king's will made known. These private fortified residences were the 'castles' of the pre-feudal nobility.

The Normans in England   Into this world burst the

18

Norman knights. Descended originally from Vikings who had settled in northern France, by the end of the 12th century they were established from Sicily in the south to Scotland in the north, and from Ireland in the west to the Holy Land in the east. The word *knight* is curiously enough not a Norman one, but Saxon—it means simply a young man; and initially the Norman knights were merely men (vassals) bound to serve as cavalrymen. *Chivalry* at this stage meant men who fought on horseback (the origin of our word 'cavalry'), and hence came to denote a code of behaviour appropriate to such men. It was a code of war, not of peace, and only in its later days did it cover the behaviour of men towards women.

The Norman knight held his land in return for serving his lord as a cavalryman. He was also required to advise his lord in court, to safeguard his interests, and to refrain from injuring him in any way. In return, his lord agreed to assist him if attacked, to stand by him in court, and to arbitrate between him and his fellow knights in the event of a dispute. This 'contract', which combined personal, military and economic relationships, was the basis of feudal society. As the knight owed service to his lord, and received assistance from him, so did his lord owe service to the king and expected assistance in return.

This hierarchy of personal loyalties determined the way in which the castles built by these men were used. It was through their castles that the Normans gained control of England, and it was through their castles that their descendants kept that control and extended it to Wales, Scotland and Ireland. According to later legal theory, the right of an individual to build a castle was delegated by the king, who had inherited the state monopoly on fortification imposed by the Romans. Seen in this light, no castle was completely private. Castles built by Norman barons to guard the lands they

19

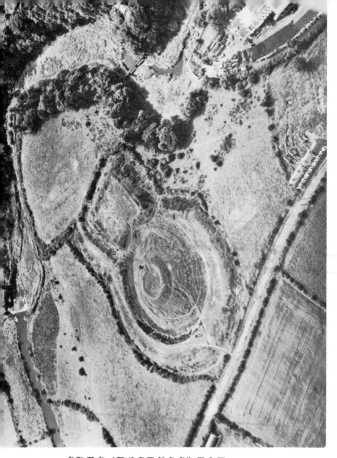

The earthworks of a motte and bailey castle at Dromore, Co. Down: all that remains of a once substantial wooden fort of the type used in the conquest of England and subsequently of Ireland

had been given thus extended the king's power, but only for so long as he could enforce the feudal 'contract'. On occasions when there were rival claimants to the throne, the system of service to an individual rather than to the state caused chaos; loyalties became blurred, and each baron sought to enhance his own position during the confusion. Castles then became private bargaining counters, chess-pieces in the game of war, symbols of political ambition and pretension.

Sporadic outbreaks of revolt and subsequent repression during the first two centuries of Norman rule produced a monstrous crop of castles. Some were built according to a strategic plan; William the Conqueror planted castles in every major Saxon town in the years following 1066, and Stephen blockaded the Isle of Ely in 1140 by planting castles around the edge of the fens. Others were built singly in response to some local emergency; thus in 1165–7 Henry II built Orford Castle in Suffolk in response to the revolt of the Earl of Norfolk. For the most part, however, castles were built as fortified country seats of the new Norman aristocracy, and their distribution reflects the economic interests of their owners rather than any grand concept of strategy.

By the 13th century the main pattern of castle building in England was complete. Shifting allegiances among the barons might result here and there in the rebuilding of a castle on a grander scale; the enrichment of a hitherto politically unimportant family by war or marriage might lead to a demand for an appropriate status symbol; but it was the 13th-century invasions of Wales and Scotland on the one hand, and the Crusades to the Holy Land on the other, which spurred the later development of the medieval castle.

Wales The Normans moved into Wales relatively early from Marcher lordships based on Monmouth, Montgomery and Chester. By 1090 Earl Hugh of

Chester had reached the shores of the Menai Straits, and Cardigan (the subject of a Norman raid early in the 1070s) had a Norman settlement backed by a castle by 1093. Bernard of Neufmarché had pushed through to Brecon in mid Wales by 1094, and there was a steady penetration of the southern plain of Glamorgan throughout the later 11th century.

Royal control of the castles built by Norman lords in Wales must always have been remote, and most of the castles built during the 12th and early 13th centuries were the response by lords both Welsh and Norman to local confrontations. The last decades of the 13th century, however, saw one of the most remarkable campaigns of strategic castle building in Europe.

In 1277 the last native Prince of Wales, Llewelyn ap Gruffydd, broke the uneasy truce between the two countries. The punitive expedition mounted by Edward I was intensified after Llywelyn's death in a skirmish in 1282. What followed was a deliberate attempt by Edward to bring Wales firmly under the control of the English crown. Between 1277 and 1297 ten royal and four baronial castles were begun with all the resources that the English feudal state could muster. Motive, means and opportunity combined to produce some of the most prodigiously powerful castles ever built. Never again would these circumstances combine to such a degree, nor would the function of the medieval castle as the instrument of royal control be so vigorously expressed. Caernarvon in particular, with its echoes of the old imperial city of Constantinople, was intended to mark the dawning of a new age in Wales, in which further castle building by the English would not be necessary, and by the Welsh would not be tolerated. In the event, it was not until a century and a half later that anything on this scale was even attempted in Wales.

22

A reconstruction by Alan Sorrell of Edward I's castle at Conway, Gwynedd, as it must have appeared about the year 1300

Scotland   No account of British castles should omit a reference to the *brochs* of Scotland. What form of society it was that produced these graceful dry-stone towers in about the 1st century AD is far from clear, but it is unlikely to have been feudal in the medieval sense. For this reason it is perhaps unwise to term the brochs 'castles' in the sense that Caernarvon is so called. Nevertheless, they show that the principle of the isolated defensive tower or keep is an old one, and not necessarily the product of a feudal society.

Following the Norman Conquest of England, border raiding led to Norman settlement in Lowland Scotland. Scottish kings such as Alexander I encouraged the establishment of Normans under feudal tenure, and the south western lands in particular, where the royal power was weaker, saw an eruption of private castle building at the turn of the 11th century.

Working out the date when a castle was built in Scotland is often difficult, since there was less use of written documents than in England—or, at least, fewer have survived from the medieval period. Moreover, because good freestone was scarce, and many sites were already defended by nature, castles were often simple in design and devoid of diagnostic features which might aid the historian or archaeologist. Where adequate evidence does exist, however, it would seem to suggest that the Norman and Scots lords of the Lowlands at least kept abreast of contemporary developments in castle building. Along the western seaboard, however, lie castles which reflect the struggles of the Scottish kings to extend their influence over areas formerly under Norse control. These castles may date from the 13th century or even later; but in appearance they resemble the castles of the late 11th or early 12th centuries in England. Although castles are known to have been built throughout the 12th and early 13th centuries by the Norse, few surviving castles can be certainly attributed to them.

24

Uncertainty about their builders similarly attends the great castles of the later 13th century. The invasions of the English King Edward I saw much building and rebuilding of castles, in which it is difficult to disentangle the work of successive Scots and English lords. 127, 128

The failure of Edward I to impose a lasting peace in Scotland left as a legacy three centuries of border warfare, lasting until the union of the two crowns in 1603. Warfare brought its inevitable consequence, however, and after the climacteric of Edward's wars few Scottish lords could afford to build the great fortresses demanded by contemporary military fashion. The 14th and 15th centuries saw the evolution of a type of keep—the 'peel' or 'tower house'—more appropriate to the reduced resources and needs of the feudal aristocracy. Since the effective power of the state developed more slowly in Scotland than in England, partly because many kings came to the throne as minors, the tower house was retained and elaborated long after such works had been abandoned in England and Wales. 129, 130
152

Ireland In Ireland, as in Scotland and Wales, the earliest Norman castles were built against a background of earlier, simpler fortifications, the 'castles' of the pre-feudal native aristocracy, whose internal dissension had provided the opportunity for Norman intervention in the 1160s. Thereafter the pattern of castle building followed that seen in England, Wales and Scotland, though offset by a century from the date of the Norman conquest of England.

In a place as remote from the English royal court as Ireland, royal control was difficult to maintain, and the Norman lords in Ireland achieved a degree of independence vastly greater than that achieved in Wales and Scotland. To be sure, there were royal attempts to regain control, and King John was forced to lay siege to one of the castles of the self-styled Earl of Ulster, John

25

The unsettled state of Scottish politics in the 15th century is shown by Sir William Borthwick's keep-like tower house at Borthwick in Lothian, built in the 1430s

de Courcy, in an attempt to assert at least the theory of feudal overlordship.

As in the early stages of the conquest of England and Wales a century earlier, much use was initially made of castles of earth and timber. They were built not according to any overall strategic plan, but rather to protect the homes of individual lords and to form the visible centre of their new landholdings. These early castles sometimes incorporated the earthworks of the residences of the native aristocracy—possibly indicating that in all the confusion of war at least the old administrative centres were retained.

157, 190

158

The castles were clustered most thickly, as might be expected, along the line of the interface between Norman and Irish territory. As this frontier moved westwards in the 13th century, so it left behind it to the east the fossilized frontiers of earlier stages: as it retreated eastwards in the 15th century it left the outlying castles 'stranded' among the Irish.

The Irish chiefs were not slow to copy the castles of the invaders, possibly for reasons of prestige as much as anything else. As in Scotland and Wales, the 'habit of vertical building', which characterized early Norman military architecture, was taken up avidly and with it, it would seem, the association of lordship with the strong tower.

Tower houses thus came to characterize Irish and Anglo-Irish castles in the 15th century as they did castles in Scotland, and probably for the same reason—they were the most appropriate form of fortified dwelling for a lord of limited means who feared the sudden raid more than the formal siege; and, as in Scotland, the type was retained and elaborated for as long as such conditions continued.

161, 169
170

Cost and Resources   The form and extent of a castle represented a compromise between three conflicting factors: the desire for comfort, the need for security, and the resources available for the job. An earthwork castle of the sort used by the Normans during the early years of conquest in England, and later (in much the same circumstances) in Wales, Scotland and Ireland, was relatively quick and cheap to build. The operative word here is 'relatively'—earthwork castles could be made from materials ready to hand with largely unskilled labour, whereas stone castles might require the transport of materials and certainly the use of more skilled craftsmen. Royal accounts of the middle of the 12th century show that a great stone tower or keep such as that at Newcastle-upon-Tyne might cost £1000, spread over the nine years of building. The keep at Dover cost more than £3000, but this was exceptional; Henry II built himself a complete new castle at Orford for £1400. Most impressive of all the 12th-century castles was Château Gaillard in Normandy, the masterpiece of Richard I, and his favourite castle. Built extraordinarily quickly in a mere three years, the castle cost over £11,000. Half of this sum was spent on getting materials—stone, lime, timber, iron and ropes—and on bringing them to the chosen site; the other half of the money was spent on the actual construction of the castle.

These sums must be weighed against the resources available at the time. When Château Gaillard was built at a cost of £11,000, less than a dozen English barons had an income of more than £400 per year, and of these the richest had no more than £800. A knight might live quite comfortably on an annual income of £20. The total ordinary revenues available to the crown for private use and for affairs of state (including defence) did not exceed £12,000 per year at that time. Yet Henry II and his son Richard I often spent one tenth or more of this each year on castle building.

A century later, when prices had risen, Edward I

spent enormous sums on his great Welsh castles. Harlech cost £9500, Conway £14,000 and Caernarvon a staggering £27,000—though this last sum was spread over a good many years. In all, Edward probably spent about £100,000 in twenty-five years of intensive castle building in Wales. To convert them to present day values, it would be necessary to multiply these sums by a factor of at least three hundred.

The details of Edward's building programme are recorded in some detail in the royal accounts. Huge numbers of men were employed each summer. At Harlech in 1286 the average weekly labour force was 100 men: Harlech, Conway and Caernarvon between them employed 2500. Beaumaris was a 'rush job', and for this 3500 men were employed during the summer of 1295.

The gathering of such numbers of men was a major task in itself, and the prodigious efforts made to secure an adequate work force showed clearly the importance set by Edward on his new castles. Craftsmen and labourers could be conscripted for the king's work, though they had to be paid. Thus ditchers were rounded up in Norfolk, Suffolk and the Fenlands; masons from the Cotswolds, Yorkshire and the West Midlands; and carpenters from all the Midland counties. Parties of men were escorted across England by the royal officers, assembling at Chester before moving on to the construction sites. Iron for fittings and timber for scaffolding were sent by sea from the Forest of Dean. Most important of all, money was raised in various parts of the country and sent under security guard for the payment of wages on site.

This last item often presented difficulties when consignments of money failed to arrive in time. At Builth in Wales, work on a new royal castle stopped suddenly in August 1282 'for want of money'. Twenty-one years later, during his Scottish wars, Edward was to find his sheriffs unable to provide the 60 carpenters and 200

ditchers required for work on the new castle at Dun-
fermline, since the men concerned complained that they
had not been paid for earlier work at Linlithgow. Nor
were such labour disputes new even then: the Bayeux
Tapestry (an almost contemporary record of the Norman Conquest) shows two of the workmen employed
to build Hastings Castle settling a difference with their
shovels.

Building work was usually limited to the summer
months, when materials could be moved more easily
and mortar would set more quickly. Under these conditions, while an earthwork castle might take six to nine
months to construct, a stone castle could take as many
years. Thus, Henry II's new castle at Orford took eight
years to complete, Dover ten years, and this seems to
have been about the average as regards speed of construction. Château Gaillard was most unusual in being
completed in three years—Caernarvon was still unfinished after forty-five years!

The Decline of the Castle   Consideration of the
ever-increasing cost of building castles, in terms of both
money and time, helps to explain why they ceased to
be built. Consideration of their function explains why
most of those already built ceased to be occupied.

A castle was essentially a house, the home of its lord.
During the Middle Ages social and political conditions
demanded that a lord should use his house as a weapon.
By the 14th century, however, developments in warfare had made a truly impregnable castle beyond the
means of most men, however rich. The invention of
gunpowder played little part in this: not until the following century were guns powerful enough to breach
a castle wall. English society was changing, however,
and men demanded more comfort in their houses—if
necessary, at the expense of security. Even the battles
of the Wars of the Roses (1455–87), a time when some
30

A realization of the true potential of artillery is shown by Henry VIII's gun forts, such as this one at Deal in Kent, seen here as reconstructed (on paper, at least) by Alan Sorrell

great lords held excessive power, were fought for the most part in open country, not round castles, and by the end of the 15th century the change was complete. Castles went out of use simply because the form of society which produced them had itself become defunct. Army officers occupied Henry VIII's new gun forts because they were paid to do so, not because the forts were their homes. A strong monarchy ensured internal peace, and while the nobility continued to build great houses for themselves, these were no longer fortified.

In Scotland and Ireland such conditions did not obtain until much later, and so castles continued to be built and occupied throughout the 16th and 17th centuries. In particular, many of the best known castles of Scotland date from this period. Elsewhere however, the need for private fortification had vanished, and while some castles continued to be occupied by their owners for reasons of sentiment or tradition, others fell into disuse and decay. It is ironic that in so many cases it should be the State which now preserves them, for it was the gradual emergence of the idea of the State in the later Middle Ages which brought about their demise.

III THE DEVELOPMENT
OF THE MEDIEVAL CASTLE

When the Normans invaded England in 1066 the idea of private fortification (i.e., castles as opposed to fortified towns) was still quite new, and very few types of building had been evolved specifically for the purpose. The Conquest itself, however, brought together men from many parts of Europe—from Normandy and Brittany, Flanders and Anjou, even perhaps from Southern Italy. Each of these areas had its own traditions of fortification. There followed a virtual explosion of castle building in which new ideas were tried out and, if found successful, were quickly applied elsewhere. Fortification by rampart and ditch gave way to complex constructions of stone with high walls, towers, battlements and a host of ingenious devices aimed at deterring an attacker. Many of these ideas had already been developed by the Romans a thousand years earlier. Much of the history of medieval castle building is the history of the rediscovery or reinvention of old techniques.

Castles of the Conquest When the Normans landed at Pevensey their immediate need was for rapidly constructed bases from which their cavalry could operate. (It has been claimed that the prefabricated parts of timber castles were brought over from Normandy. No chronicles of that time mention this, but prefabricated castles were certainly taken to Ireland a hundred years later.) After William's coronation the need was for royal garrison posts in all the major towns. At the same time knights and barons settling down in

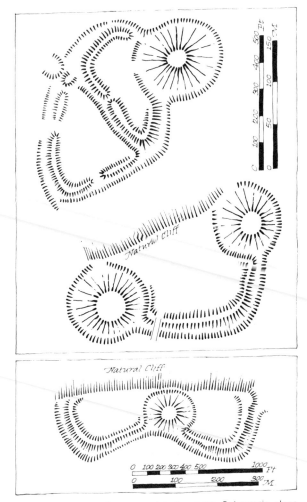

Earthwork castles of motte and bailey type. Schematic plans based on Brinklow and Lewes (top) and Windsor (bottom)

the countryside to enjoy the lands given them as spoils of war needed some means to protect themselves against sudden uprisings. Speed was vital, and so the earliest castles built by the Normans were constructed from materials available close at hand—i.e., from timber and earth. Nearly 100 castles are known to have been built by the time of the great Domesday inquiry in 1086, and these were almost all of earth and timber.

The most common form of earthwork castle was that known as the **motte and bailey.** The main buildings— 65, 77 hall, kitchen, chapel, stables, barn—were grouped 134, 157 within a courtyard (the 'bailey') protected by a rampart and ditch, the rampart being fronted by a palisade of timber. Overlooking the bailey was a huge pile of earth (the 'motte') supporting a timber tower and again fronted by a palisade. Occasionally, however, the motte is missing, the element of height being provided by a tall timber gatehouse, and it may be that these simpler castles, known as **ringworks,** represent an older type 30, 64 of Norman castle, before the motte was invented. 74

Earthwork castles present the modern visitor with something of a problem, for while the earth banks remain to impress us by their size, it was probably the timbering which took the eye in the 11th century. Indeed, it may be wrong to think of earthwork castles as fundamentally different from those built of stone. In some cases, at least, the earth was revetted in timber; wood was plastered and painted to look like stone. It is possible, therefore, that earthwork castles were just cheap versions of stone ones. The rotting away of the timber facing has left exposed the earth core, which has then been eroded by wind and rain to give a profile much less dramatic than that of a stone wall or tower. The difference might not have been so apparent in the 11th century.

Such, then, were the castles of the Conquest. For all their simplicity, they were effective against surprise

35

attack, and the towers on the high mottes dominated the landscape, announcing the arrival of a new regime. How effective they were is shown by their widespread use in England, Wales and Scotland, and by the fact that when the Normans moved on to Ireland in the late 1160s the motte and bailey castle—by then almost obsolete in Britain—was revived and used extensively in conditions that closely resembled those of the conquest of England a century earlier.

The Period of Consolidation   While the earthwork castle might be made to look like a stone castle, it was much more vulnerable to attack by fire, and great efforts were made to replace the timberwork with stone as soon as conditions and resources allowed.

Since any attack was usually concentrated on the baileygate in the first instance, this was often rebuilt first,
4, 43 in the form of a stone tower. Sliding gates and draw-
64 bridges completed the protection of what was otherwise the weakest point in the defences. (At this stage the drawbridge was simply a bridge which could be withdrawn: lifting bridges came later.)

10, 16 Palisades, too, were replaced in stone to form **curtain**
60 **walls,** although many castles still had timber-palisaded baileys in the 13th century. To increase the effectiveness of the curtain wall, provision was often made for the erection of overhanging wooden galleries (*hourds*) along the parapet. Factors controlling the conversion of timber palisades into stone were the availability of good building stone (or the proximity of a river along which stone could be transported), finance and local military need, and it is difficult to see any strategic pattern determining which castles were first rebuilt in stone.

As the palisades around the bailey were rebuilt in
4, 79 stone, so too were those around the summits of the
90 mottes. In such **shell keeps** it is often possible to see

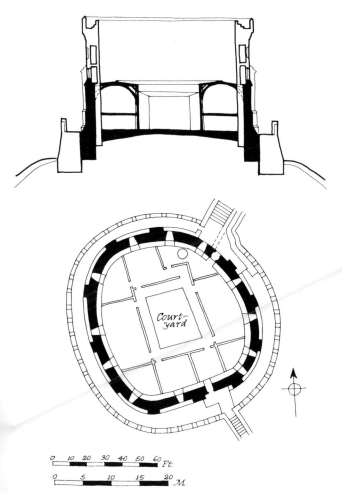

64, 75 where timber or stone buildings were ranged against
84 the inner face of the new wall, leaving an open space at the centre. Shell keeps occur sporadically during the 12th century: their very simplicity makes it difficult to determine when individual examples were built, and it is not possible to say for how long the idea re-
147 mained fashionable in England and Wales. In Scotland, shell keeps were still being built in the 13th century.

Curtain and Keep Not every castle went through this process of 'timber into stone'. If good stone was ready to hand, castles might be built in this material from the start. Where they survive, these early stone castles
30, 46 give to the **gatehouse** a prominence far beyond what
66 was necessary for military purposes alone. It is possible that the reasons for this lie in an association of a tall gate-house with rights of justice and lordship—an association going back to the 9th and 10th centuries (it may not be entirely coincidental that the great west portals of Norman cathedral churches were the setting for sculpted scenes of judgement).

These early castles with their stone gatehouses and curtain walls are the stone counterparts of the earthen ringworks with their timber gatehouses and palisades. They represent a tradition in castle building which runs throughout the Middle Ages, though eclipsed for a while by a shift of emphasis to the motte and its stone counterpart, the keep.

Rivalling the gatehouse in importance—though for different reasons—was the **hall.** This, the formal centre of the medieval household, similarly carried overtones of lordship, since it was here that the lord of the castle would preside in court or council. By the eve of the Conquest, bitter experience on the Continent had shown the value of building one's hall in stone, and of setting it at first-floor level. Such a building was both fireproof and capable of being defended should the

38

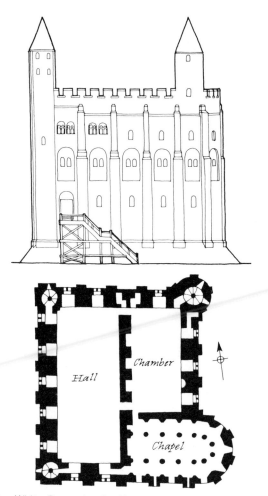

The White Tower in the Tower of London. Elevation of S side and plan of main residential floor

bailey defences be stormed. Stone halls at first-floor level
thus appear in some early English castles and may once
have been more common. A necessary ancillary to the
formal and public hall was the private chamber. Placed
side by side at first-floor level, hall and chamber formed
a compact block of masonry capable of containing
most, if not all, of the space necessary for the lord's
household. Herein lay the genesis of the **keep**—a fortified house of more than one storey, incorporating hall,
chamber and chapel, standing foursquare within its
bailey and forming a final place of refuge.

Experiments were made with this form during the
first decades after the Conquest, and the basic type continued to be built well into the 12th century. Even that
most famous 'keep' of all—the White Tower, which
gives its name to the Tower of London—is of this hall
and chamber type, though magnified to the proportions
appropriate to the residence of the Conqueror.

With the 12th century, however, came an increasing
insistence on height, possibly as the lessons learned during the wars between Henry I and his brother Duke
Robert of Normandy at the beginning of that century
were translated into stone. The new keeps were taller,
having three or more storeys, and the stairs leading up
to their entrances were enclosed within forebuildings.
In some cases, earlier lower buildings were heightened
to meet the new requirements. Elsewhere, great towers
were built from scratch, mainly at royal or episcopal
command, but also by the richer barons: the death of
Henry I in 1135 brought a disputed succession, and a
number of baronial keeps probably belong to the subsequent period known as the Anarchy, 'when men said
openly that Christ and his saints slept'.

The restoration of royal authority under Henry II
from 1154 saw the building of some notable keeps with
increasingly sophisticated interior planning, culminat-
ing in the building of the royal keep at Dover during
40

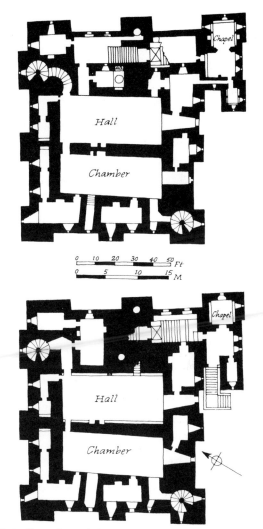

Dover: floor plans of the upper (top) and lower (bottom) suites in the keep

the 1180s. This great block of masonry measured 29×28 m (95×91 ft) in plan, rising some 28 m (91 ft) high, with walls up to 6 m (19 ft) thick. Within this palatial cube were two main floors providing accommodation, above a basement. Each main floor was served by a separate chapel, contrived in the forebuilding over the entrance stairs and thus perhaps adding the protection of God to that afforded by drawbridge and barred door. Above ground-floor level—and thus beyond the reach of battering rams—the walls were built hollow to provide small chambers which might serve as closets, bed-chambers, wardrobes and the like. Latrines were similarly set in narrow passages running in the thickness of the walls. A well enabled water to be drawn to the second floor whence it was piped to various parts of the building—though in this sophistication Dover seems to have been unique.

But not every keep formed so self-contained a residence, however. Some are devoid of fireplaces, which is a sure sign that the lord of the castle did not envisage a great deal of time being spent in the keep, which thus served as a place of temporary refuge rather than as a house.

At the same time that Dover was being built as the largest and most expensive keep of its day, experiments were being made with other ground plans. Circular ground plans, giving cylindrical towers, are known from the middle of the 12th century. By the end of that century the fashion for such cylindrical keeps was all-pervading. Wales in particular, where the deteriorating military situation of that time necessitated new major works, saw a plethora of such keeps. The change is usually attributed to a determination to eliminate projecting corners, since these were vulnerable to bombardment and mining alike. An example often quoted is Rochester, where King John rebuilt in rounded form the corner of the keep he had undermined and brought crashing down during the siege of 1215. Nevertheless, keeps continued to be built from square and rectangular ground plans well into the 13th century, particularly in Ireland; and, indeed, it can be argued that the rectangular keep was never really forgotten so long as castles needed to be built. The choice between curved and rectilinear forms was thus not dictated solely by military needs, nor does it reflect a simple chronological succession. Fashion, the availability of freestone for corners and the type of accommodation planned within the building must also have been taken into account. 160, 184 190

The 12th century thus witnessed the rise of the keep. Keeps were built in rectilinear or curved forms throughout the remaining centuries of the Middle Ages and continued to serve a lower level of society in Scotland and Ireland at least until the 17th century. However, experience in attacking castles, whether gained in Britain, France or the Holy Land, led to a growing realization that passive defence was not enough. The later 12th and 13th centuries saw increasing efforts being made to keep attackers away from the base of the keep and indeed out of the bailey altogether. Even so, while new building might concentrate on gatehouse and curtain wall, most castles in existence by 1300 boasted a keep of some sort, even if only one 'left over' from the 12th century. 33, 48 80

Wall Towers   The translation into stone of a wooden palisade might make it fireproof: it did not necessarily make it more effective as an obstacle. Once an attacker had crossed the ditch and gained the foot of the wall it was difficult for a defender to dislodge him without leaning so far over the parapet as to expose himself to the fire of archers still standing on the other side of the ditch. Two solutions were adopted. The simpler was to 'bend' the curtain wall into a series of projecting rectangular salients from which counter-fire could be

Late 13th-century wall towers at Conway, Gwynedd

directed along the outer face of the wall. The earliest surviving example of this approach is Carisbrooke on the Isle of Wight, a work of the 1120s. Long before this, however, the practice was known of incorporating towers into the curtain wall in such a way that they projected forward from its line. By the 1160s and 1170s towers were beginning to be placed sufficiently close to each other as to afford mutual protection, each tower serving to cover the 'dead ground' of its neighbour. In this they revived ideas already fully developed during the later Roman Empire. They may also have borrowed from designs tried out in timber during the intervening centuries, examples of which no longer survive. Certainly, walls interrupted by projecting towers were

44

to be seen in many parts of England, France and Spain, whether protecting abandoned Roman forts or revived Roman cities, and it seems strange that the advantages of the design took so long to be appreciated. 63, 80 90

The advantage of the wall tower was that, in addition to providing the opportunity to direct flanking fire along the outer face of the curtain, it could be built high to command the wall head itself, in case this should be taken. It also formed something of a redoubt should the bailey be overrun and the defenders unable to escape into the keep. The effect of such building was to increase the defensive fire power of the castle to such a degree as to make it almost offensive. From arrow-loops at ground level, from the wall head, and from the tower top archers could pour a withering fire on troops gathering for an attack. Simple assault became a hazardous undertaking, and new methods of attack had to be devised.

The earliest wall towers to survive are rectangular in plan, suggesting a derivation from timber originals. By the early 13th century, however, rounded forms were 8, 27 being introduced, echoing the change made in the prevalent form of the keep a generation or so earlier. As with the keep, however, rounded forms never completely ousted rectangular ones, and it was the disposition of the wall towers rather than their form which determined their effectiveness.

Gatehouses This emphasis on the defence of the curtain brought a renewed concern for the protection of the gate, potentially always the weakest point of the defences. Hitherto the entry into a castle had been through a passage contrived in a square tower, which thus became a gatehouse, and the early association of the tall gatehouse with the idea of lordship has been 27 noted. Henry II's new works at Dover in the 1180s show a new idea being born. The entrances into the inner bailey were set between closely spaced pairs of wall towers from which fire could be brought to bear on those attacking the gates. The next stage, achieved by the 1220s, was to join the towers on each side of the gateway with a linking room above the gate passage, so forming a single twin-towered structure. (Here again the medieval castle builder had arrived at a solution adopted by Roman military architects a thousand years earlier.) Once invented—or rediscovered—this type of gatehouse continued to be built with square, rounded or polygonal projecting towers until the end of the Middle Ages and beyond.

8, 82

It is over the gate, towards the end of the 13th century, that we find the earliest British examples of **machicolation,** the replacement in stone of the temporary timber 'hourds' which were applied to keep and curtain wall alike during the 12th century. Further protection was provided by adding a small outer enclosure or **barbican** with its own gate, lying beyond the main ditch and often encircled by a ditch of its own.

82, 99

33, 80
190

Wall tower, barbican and gatehouse enabled the defenders of a castle to keep the enemy at a distance—so long as he remained above ground. The enemy below ground presented a greater problem. Undermining by tunnelling was, in the long run, the most effective way of bringing down a wall or tower. To combat this it was necessary to raise the natural water-table in the vicinity of the castle, so that any tunnel would automatically flood, drowning the miners. This was the original purpose of the castle **moat.** There were of course, other advantages to be gained from it. A moat made it difficult for an attacker to bring ladders and wooden assault towers close to the castle walls. It provided a supply of water in case of fire. It could even be stocked with fish. But primarily it existed to discourage tunnelling.

By the first quarter of the 13th century the main ele-

A machicolated gatehouse of the late 14th century: Bodiam in Sussex

ments of English castle building—curtain and wall tower, keep, gatehouse and moat—had been assembled. Few castles showed any great regularity in the disposition of these elements, most having been pieced together by the twin processes of adoption and adaption. Further development could come only when motive and means for new building could be found.

The Concentric Castle Motive and means were found most dramatically in connection with Edward I's Welsh wars at the end of the 13th century, when

47

completely new castles of royal or even 'national' status were required and when the full resources of one of the richest countries in Western Europe could be put to their building.

Rarely can foreign influence be identified so readily as it can in Edward's Welsh castles. From 1270 to 1272 the future king was on crusade in the Holy Land. What he learned there cannot be asertained, though it would appear that he was struck by the 4th-century walls of Constantinople, since the walls of his castle of Caernarvon were later modelled on them to enhance echoes of imperial rule enshrined in local legend. What is known, however, is that on his way home he called on his greatuncle, Philip I of Savoy, and there met Philip's architect,

Caernarvon: Edward I's attempt to capture the imperial echoes of Constantinople

Master James of St George. This man became Edward's master builder and had a hand in almost every major castle built by Edward during the next two decades.

The most dramatic of Edward's Welsh castles are those which rise from irregular rocky sites. All the elements of fortification developed by earlier generations are here concentrated in a frightening display of 'over-kill'. More enlightening perhaps are the castles built on flat ground, since here the will of the architect was dominant, not the terrain. Rhuddlan, Beaumaris and Harlech show what has been called the 'concentric plan of fortification' in that the buildings of the castle are protected by two closely spaced curtain walls, the outer overlooked and protected by the inner. Beaumaris, the latest of Edward's Welsh castles, shows a ruthless regularity of design and can justly be called a piece of military precision engineering. Gone is the keep; the lordly accommodation is contained within twin gatehouses of massive size. Huge wall towers dominate the inner curtain and command a narrow strip of ground between it and the lower outer curtain. A moat encompasses the whole.

The idea of such 'concentric' fortification was not entirely new at this time. It had been used by the Egyptians 2000 years before the birth of Christ, and achieved its most monumental form in the Theodosian land walls of Constantinople in the 4th century AD. The walls of Constantinople were first seen by western knights in the 1090s during the First Crusade, yet they were not copied in Britain until after the Eighth Crusade almost 200 years later. Once again, it would seem that earlier precedent went ignored until medieval man had gone through his own slow process of trial and error.

The principles applied in Edward's Welsh castles can be found elsewhere, though rarely on so vast a scale. The royal castles in Wales show what could be achieved by the medieval military architect in exceptional

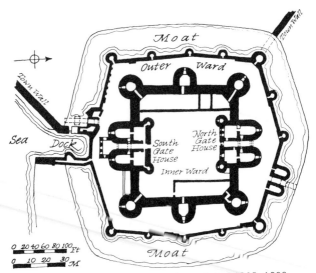

Beaumaris, Anglesey: a 'concentric castle' of 1295–1300

circumstances. Elsewhere the opportunity for complete rebuilding, as for building anew, was rarely present, and most often a compromise had to be made between what was fashionable and what was inherited from earlier generations. Only in Scotland, where Edward directed his energies after 1295, were castles built on anything approaching the scale of the royal works in Wales.

The Later Middle Ages   Not even Edward I could afford to build castles continuously on such a scale. The 14th century saw a levelling off in castle building, if only because most of the needs of kings and barons had by then been met. As money became available individual lords rebuilt the more outdated parts of their castles, but even so many castles remained very simple in form throughout the Middle Ages.

89, 113
24, 80
84
127 128
132
10, 16
61

50

The French Wars of 1337–1453 enriched some families sufficiently for them to aspire to a more lordly residence than had hitherto been possible, and hence we occasionally find at this time new castles being built 14, 55 which embodied the newest techniques. However, the vaunting ambition of a family which has just 'arrived' can best be seen slightly later at Raglan, where in the 121 1460s Sir William Herbert—newly created Chief Justice and Chamberlain of South Wales in return for his support of the victorious House of York—built one of the most stupendous castles of the later Middle Ages. Significantly, Sir William chose to emphasize his new-found status by reviving the old idea of the keep as the most appropriate form of residence for a magnate: a keep hexagonal in plan and crowned with a massive machicolation.

This revival of the keep would at first glance seem surprising, given the direction taken by castle builders of the 13th century. However, even Edward I's castles sometimes include a keep, and the long-standing sym- 107 bolic association of the keep with the trappings of lord-ship continued to influence building practice during the 14th and 15th centuries. Thus, where new castles were required or old ones rebuilt during this period some form of strong tower is usually to be found, though few of these latter-day keeps had the defensive capabilities of 12th-century Rochester or Dover. The desire for real comfort, combined with the appearance of strength, took precedence over military zeal. In some cases even the machicolations, which are such a feature of these 31, 76 towers, are bogus.

The later Middle Ages also saw the development of gunnery, and this is often held to have been a major factor in the decline of the castle. Certainly, guns attracted a great deal of attention. James II of Scotland conceived a passion for them which led to his death at Roxburgh in 1460, when 'a mis-formed gun brake in shooting, by which he was stricken to the ground and died hastily'. However, when first introduced in the early 14th century, guns were small in size and discharged only iron darts. Not until the mid-15th century were guns big enough to project missiles capable of smashing the walls of a castle under siege, and even then they were cumbersome to transport and difficult to use. By the 1370s small guns were being used for the defence of castles, and loops designed for their discharge can be found from then onwards. Apart from this, the introduction of gunnery brought about no great changes in castle building during the Middle Ages. Only Ravenscraig, built just before his death by the over-enthusiastic James II of Scotland, shows any serious attempt to adapt the castle's defences for the discharge of heavy guns. For the rest, guns took their place among catapults and crossbows, frightening friend and foe alike, but contributing little to the real business of siege warfare.

The full panoply of later medieval fortification is perhaps best seen at Warwick. Here in the 1380s Thomas Beauchamp, 12th Earl of Warwick, rebuilt the eastern facade of the castle to incorporate a great gatehouse and barbican, flanked by two huge wall towers—all in the latest French style. Elsewhere, the major building works of the 14th- and 15th-century nobility were centred on their domestic buildings. The period saw the gradual evolution of a new type of fortified house in which the formerly separate 'houses in the castle' were gathered into closely integrated ranges of buildings set round a courtyard, rather in the fashion of the contemporary but unfortified Oxford and Cambridge colleges. The exterior walls might present a more or less warlike appearance, but the natural development of this type of building was towards the great country house of the Tudor period, in which battlemented parapets, gatehouse and moat were retained as the outward symbols of wealth and power, but without serious intent.

52

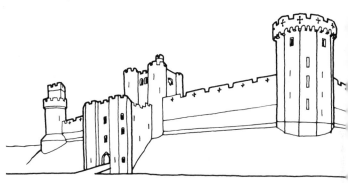

The east front of Warwick Castle, rebuilt in grandiose style in the later 14th century

By contrast, the fortifications built for national defence by the emergent State in the early 16th century took full account of the new weapons of artillery and a paid army. Nothing could demonstrate more clearly than the forms of these barrack-like gun forts the gradual but fundamental changes in society that took place at the close of the Middle Ages.

In Northern England, Scotland and Ireland, however, where raiding was almost endemic, keeps (suit- 126 ably scaled down to meet the resources available and 171, 178 often called **peels** or **tower houses** by modern historians) continued to be built in large numbers: indeed, their remains often outnumber those of the medieval 164, 190 castles which inspired them. In 1429 the government of the young Henry VI deliberately encouraged the building of small keeps within the area of English settlement in Ireland:

'It is agreed and asserted that every liegeman of our Lord the King who chooses to build within the next ten years a castle or tower sufficiently embattled or fortified, to wit 20 feet in length, 16 feet in width and 40 feet in height, the Commons of those counties shall pay to the said person to build the said castle or tower £10 by way of subsidy.'

Such towers were the bare minimum, however. English and Irish alike frequently built larger towers, usually
176 protecting a small walled yard or **bawn**. In Scotland in particular the late medieval tower house enjoyed a veritable 'Indian summer' of popularity, the simpler
126, 130 forms of the 15th century giving way to the more elaborate, even fantastic, skylines of the 16th and 17th cen-
129, 162 turies in the style familiarly known as 'Scottish Baronial' but derived from French castles of the Renaissance.

In this chapter the main trends in castle building during the Middle Ages have been described. What constitutes a castle is, and was, largely a subjective matter. A minor lord might accept as a 'castle' something his king might reject as only a 'fortified manor', and the dividing line can rarely have been clear to either. Emphasis has been laid on the private and residential aspects of the castle, yet even these can be exaggerated. Caernarvon was hardly private in any real sense and the idea of the garrison fort was never entirely absent during the Middle Ages. Nevertheless, the Middle Ages did see a unique combination of house, fort and administrative centre, and when changes in society demanded that this combination be broken up, the 'castle' ceased to exist except as an abandoned shell.

IV   CASTLES AT WAR

No matter how much money and time might be spent on building a castle, it was only a shell designed for the protection of those inside. The defenders of a castle were always more important than the castle itself. An unreduced castle might contain a field force of mounted knights; it had be made to surrender in such a way as to neutralize the striking power of the field force it contained.

Reducing a castle held by a determined garrison was an expensive undertaking. An army had to be assembled, miners recruited for tunnelling, timber felled for making assault apparatus, stone quarried for missiles, and food and water laid on for the besieging force. To put a castle on a war footing was to invite your opponent, be he king or baron, to consider the cost of all this. If he did not know the extent of the defenders' resources, the element of bluff, ever present in warfare, was increased.

If the challenge was taken up, the bluff was called. Then the defenders could only hope for one of two things: that relief would come, causing the siege to be raised; or that diversionary raids by allies elsewhere would cause the besiegers to turn their attention to their own castles. If neither happened, then slow starvation would eventually enforce surrender.

In the event, few castles were held to the bitter end. Sieges such as those of Rochester (13th October–30th November, 1215) and Bedford (June–August, 1224) were unusual, and attracted attention for that reason. After the keep of Rochester was mined and the defenders starved out by King John's forces, it was

Early Norman warfare! The motte at Dinan in Britanny is taken by Duke William in 1064. This scene from the Bayeux Tapestry shows the first cavalry charge, the attack by fire and (on the right) the surrender of the keys to the castle

hoped that 'few would put their trust in castles' (though here the medieval chronicler was over-optimistic). Nine years later, at Bedford, political motives, combined with the vast trouble he had been put to in assembling the besieging army and the casualties inflicted on it, caused the young King Henry III to hang the garrison after he had burned them out. Usually, however, a garrison might expect to march out with full honours, the game of bluff having been played according to the rules, and lost. In many cases, castles were never put to the test, but passed their days in peace, their bluff never called.

Early Tactics and Weapons By and large, earthwork castles were not expected to withstand protracted sieges. Long sieges did occur in the 11th century: the young Duke William (later to be called the Conqueror) took two years to starve his uncle out of the Castle of

DINANTES: ET: CVNAN: CLAVES: PORREXIT: HIC: WILLELM: DEDIT: HAROLDO ARMA

Arques in Normandy, and the defenders of Brionne held out on their island in the river for three years. But these were exceptional cases. Earthwork castles of the 11th and 12th centuries were designed rather to withstand surprise attacks, and in particular to withstand the onset of cavalry. Even so, the timber defences of ringworks and the baileys of motte and bailey castles were limited in height and vulnerable to attack by fire. The high motte was more defensible, but it afforded a very limited space for men and provisions, and it was useless for the protection of the vital horses.

The 'hit-and-run' nature of early castle warfare is shown with all the vividness of a contemporary strip cartoon on the Bayeux Tapestry, commissioned to celebrate the conquest of England and made within the lifetime of those who took part in it. The attack on the Breton Castle of Dinan in particular shows the full sequence of the sudden appearance of the Norman cavalry, the defence of the timber gate leading through the palisade round the summit of the motte, the attempt by two dismounted knights—once the surprise attack by cavalry had failed—to set fire to the timbers of the palisade, and finally the surrender of the castle, with its keys held out on a lance. The strength and weakness of the earth-and-timber castle are here made plain.

Fire was the main weapon of attack once the element of surprise had been lost, and against it the covering of exposed timbers with wet hides had only a limited effect. The necessity for replacing timber palisades with stone curtain walls as soon as the opportunity offered could hardly be more clear.

Once a castle had been provided with stone defences, then new methods of attack had to be devised. Chain mail was proof against sword cuts, but not against a well aimed bolt from a crossbow, and a good archer sheltered behind the battlements of a stone curtain wall or tower could pick off enough of the besiegers to discourage those remaining. Large wicker or hide-covered shields (called *pavises*) and movable huts (called *mantlets*) were necessary to protect the attacking force. Behind these, ladders could be brought up for direct assault and timber towers (known as *belfreys*) could be assembled. From these last, archers could fire over the curtain wall and—if the towers were brought close enough—attackers could leap onto the wall head itself without having to endure a perilous ascent by ladder. To move such towers close to the walls, the ditches had first to be filled with bundles of brushwood or anything else that came to hand.

A simpler, though possibly more hazardous procedure was to attack the gates by battering-ram or by fire. The increasing emphasis on the defence of the gate by elaborate flanking towers and barbicans in the 13th century bears witness to many earlier desperate but unrecorded hand-to-hand engagements round splintered and burning wooden gates.

The *ram*, sheltered beneath its protecting cover (or 'cat'), could also be used, though more laboriously, on the walls themselves. Even slower was the *bore* (or 'mouse'), a pointed ram, which nibbled away at exposed corners. Slowest of all was the use of crowbar and pick. One account of a Norse assault on a castle in Scotland relates how the stone defences were attacked with axes!

In the last resort, it was always possible to blockade a castle, starving its defenders into submission. For such protracted operations a more comfortable base for the besiegers was necessary, and temporary *siege-castles* were built. These might be of earth and timber, or they might incorporate an existing building which could be modified for the purpose. In some cases church towers were pressed into service in this way, much to the annoyance and disapproval of priest and bishop. Even nunneries and monasteries were sometimes taken over for warlike purposes. (The Abbot of Ramsey retaliated by setting fire to the tents of the soldiery encamped within his precinct.) Once a suitable base had been established, and pickets set round the besieged castle, the attackers had only to wait for time, the shortage of food and water, and the inevitable onset of disease to do their work for them.

Later Tactics and Weapons   From the chronicles of the 13th and 14th centuries it is possible to learn much about the methods of warfare currently in use. From illuminated manuscripts, and from the increasingly detailed royal accounts, a picture can be built up of the weapons themselves.

The main methods of attack were: (i) direct assault over the curtain; (ii) bombardment leading to a breach in the defences through which an assault could be made; (iii) mining; (iv) insinuation; (v) blockade; and (vi) propaganda.

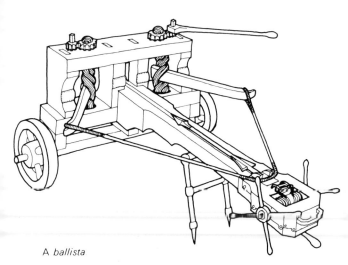

A *ballista*

Of these, direct assault still relied on the old established ladder and belfrey, ram and bore, in the use of which not much improvement could be made. Bombardment, on the other hand, was rapidly becoming more effective as machines known to the Romans and still used by the Byzantines came into use throughout the West.

The *ballista* was a form of giant crossbow mounted on a stand. It was designed for the discharge of long iron darts, and as such was primarily an anti-personnel weapon. The *mangonel*, on the other hand, was a catapult capable of hurling stones and other heavy missiles for the breaking of gates and walls. The power came from a skein of rope about the lower end of the main arm of the machine. This could be tightened and twisted by windlasses while the arm itself was locked in the lowered position and the missile placed in a cup on the end of the arm. On release the rope skein was

60

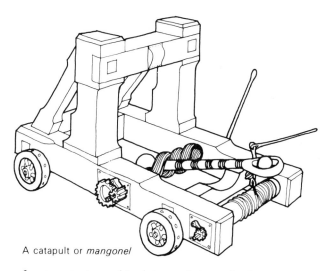

A catapult or *mangonel*

free to untwist, and in doing so it brought the arm up and over rather like a cricketer bowling a high lob.

The mangonel thus had a higher trajectory than the ballista. Its rope skein was also liable to be affected by damp. For these reasons its range was difficult to estimate, and so a second high-trajectory throwing machine was developed that relied on gravity for its power and was thus more constant in operation. This was the *trebuchet*. In the principle of its action it was rather similar to the mangonel, except that its missile was delivered from a rope sling attached to the end of the swinging arm rather than from a cup, and the arm was swung by means of a counterweight rather than by twisted ropes. The trebuchet was capable of discharging considerable loads, and was the howitzer of its day, being able to hurl a stone weighing some 150 kg (nearly 3 cwt) at least 100 m (*c.* 110 yd). A large trebuchet could hurl a dead horse!

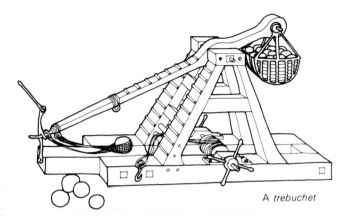

A *trebuchet*

Mangonel and trebuchet appear in the royal accounts as *petraria*, i.e., 'stone throwers'. In the field, however, they seem to have enjoyed more personal names such as Malvoisin, which means 'bad neighbour'. Indeed, the vicious business of siege warfare was concealed behind a veritable Noah's ark of animal names. Thus, walls were attacked by the 'ram' or the 'mouse', both of which sheltered beneath a 'cat' or 'sow'. The word mangonel means a 'mule' or 'nag', the machine being so named from the way it kicked up its heels on discharge. Other machines were named after successful engagements. The great belfrey made in Glasgow for Edward I in 1301 was so successful at the siege of Bothwell that it was taken (in 30 wagons) to the siege of Stirling in 1304, where it was known as 'le Bothwell'.

Of all the missiles discharged by these machines, the most dreaded was Greek Fire—a medieval version of the modern napalm bomb. Of little use against stonework, it was deadly against men and horses, or against timber gates, roofs, barns and the like. Ostensibly it was a Byzantine secret, but it was used occasionally in the

West in the later 12th and 13th centuries, though it would seem only by royal artificers.

The logical successor to the trebuchet was the gun. Guns appear as experimental ancillary weapons in the early 14th century. The French brought to the raid on Southampton in 1338 one gun, three pounds of gunpowder, and some four dozen iron darts—hardly a decisive combination. By the mid 15th century, however, the 'foul stinking bombards' were powerful enough to breach a castle wall, though few castles seem to have been taken by this method.

The most feared weapon, because it was the most effective, was the tunnel or mine. A tunnel was started out of bowshot from the castle and continued under the foundations of the wall or tower it was desired to bring down. Brushwood was then piled round the shoring and set alight. As the shores burned through they collapsed, bringing down the roof of the tunnel and robbing the wall or tower above of its foundation.

Such a tunnel brought down the corner of the keep at Rochester in 1215. On occasion, the successful completion of a tunnel was itself enough to bring about the surrender of the castle in question. The point having been made, it did not need to be proved!

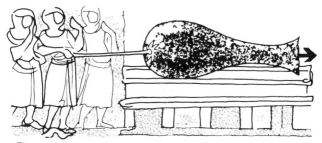

Three cautious artillery men prepare to fire an iron dart from a gun: a scene from a 14th-century manuscript

63

An altogether simpler, and apparently just as effective way of gaining entry to a castle was to insinuate a small group of men into the castle by means of a latrine chute or some other unguarded opening. Thus Château Gaillard, which represented the culmination of 12th-century castle building, was taken in 1204 by a few French soldiers who, under cover of darkness, climbed up a latrine chute and then in through a chapel window. The defenders fled, hearing the noise and thinking the whole French army had got in. To encounter unexpectedly at night someone who had just climbed up a stinking latrine shaft would indeed be an unnerving experience!

The unsavoury nature of medieval latrines could lead not merely to unpleasantness, but also to disease. In a castle under siege, disease could spell disaster. In 1088 the defenders of Rochester surrendered the castle when the smells became overpowering—presumably because the smells presaged infection.

Such conditions lay behind every blockade, and it was the hope of inducing at least the fear of them that led an attacker to initiate a blockade. A blockade was not always easy to effect, however. For one thing, the attacker could never know the quantity of provisions stored within a castle, and so could not gauge exactly how long they would last. A well provisioned castle with a good internal water supply could hold out for several months. This might prove longer than the attacker could maintain his forces in the field to operate the blockade. Apart from the sheer cost of maintaining the besieging army, there was always the possibility that his own castles or lands might be attacked in his absence. Finally, the complex nature of feudal relationships often created a confusion of loyalties, and the political situation might change radically within the time needed to starve out a well provisioned castle.

Confused loyalties could also be exploited by psychological warfare. During the siege of Kenilworth in 1266,

Prince Edward persuaded the papal legate to stand below the walls and, from a safe distance, pronounce the excommunication of the defenders. His words, we are told, were greeted with jeers and rude gestures! The garrison, by way of retaliation, dressed up their surgeon as another legate, and he in turn excommunicated Prince Edward's forces. Less dramatically, there was always the possibility that someone could be bribed to open the postern gate and let in an attacker. Harlech, otherwise almost impregnable, was taken by Owain Glyndwr in 1404 'in return for a sum of money'.

The Defence of the Castle A garrison expecting attack often attempted to strike first, ambushing their opponents in open country some distance from the castle. Thus in 1144 Geoffrey de Mandeville, Earl of Essex, seeing himself gradually being bottled up in the Isle of Ely by King Stephen's new castles round the edge of the fens, struck at the half finished castle of Burwell in an attempt to break the ring before it closed. (Unfortunately for him, it was a hot day and he had unlaced his coat of mail and tilted back his helmet. A well aimed spear terminated both his life and the attack.)

Even after the siege proper had begun, a sudden sally could bring good results, and cavalry encounters between the lines were quite common. Occasionally, such sallies proved disastrous. It was during a sally from Bamburgh Castle in 1095 that Robert de Mowbray, Earl of Northumberland, was captured by the garrison of one of William II's siege-castles. A threat to blind the Earl if Bamburgh were not surrendered brought the required submission.

Against the constant pounding of the stone-throwing engines the best defence was to build thicker walls, but this could hardly be done at short notice. Counter-barrage from stone-throwing machines mounted on top of the wall towers was more practicable. At Kenilworth in 1266 we are told that the missiles discharged by both sides often collided and splintered in mid-air, so great was the rate of fire.

The more insidious miner could best be thwarted by a moat. Failing this, recourse had to be had to the dangerous expedient of the countermine—a tunnel dug by the defenders themselves to ambush the miners of the besieging party. The terrors of a hand-to-hand struggle below ground in almost total darkness can be imagined.

Against direct assault certain measures could be taken. With the aid of long forked poles assault ladders could be pushed away from the walls and eventually toppled over. Mats could be lowered to take some of the shock of the battering ram, or an attempt could be made to catch its head with a grapnel. Timber 'hourds' erected on beams projecting from the wall head not only changed the whole appearance of a castle, giving it a more martial air, but allowed the defenders to discharge missiles and pour liquids on those below. (Boiling oil and molten lead are, alas, figments of the novelist's imagination: against a man in armour scalding water would be effective enough, and much less expensive.)

Should the attackers manage to reach the wall head, it was usually possible for the defenders to retreat into the neighbouring wall towers, which were sometimes provided with a barred door and portcullis and thus formed miniature keeps from which further defence might be conducted.

Other devices, though occasionally spectacular, had only marginal effect. Thus, at Ludlow, King Stephen and Prince Henry of Scotland were walking round the castle walls, planning their attack, when Prince Henry was neatly hooked by a grapnel dangled by one of the garrison, and was very nearly hauled up into the castle and captured. Fortunately, the King caught hold of the

Later medieval siege craft

Prince's legs and managed to hold on until the rope could be cut!

Starvation was the one form of attack which could not be countered, though it could be mitigated by strict rationing and the turning away of non-combatants. The fate of these last could be cruel. During the siege of Château Gaillard in 1204 King John's garrison was forced to drive out all non-combatants who had taken refuge in the castle. Denied access through the lines of the blockading French, the refugees starved for three winter months, even turning to cannibalism in their desperation. Eventually the few who remained were allowed through, though even these died after being given food. There was precious little 'chivalry' apparent here.

No matter how the food might be rationed it was bound to give out sooner or later. The castle must then be surrendered, unless a relieving force could break the blockade and bring fresh supplies to the starving garrison. Without such relief the garrison could only sue for whatever terms it could get. Usually, these were honourable: the cases of the starved refugees at Château Gaillard and of the hanged garrison at Bedford were exceptional. Often terms were agreed in principle well before the food ran out. At Kenilworth the garrison eventually offered to surrender the castle, which they had held for over four months, if relief was not forthcoming within 40 days. The offer was accepted, and when the time was up and relief had not been sent, the castle was duly surrendered. The '40-day' period was a common arrangement, and derived from the basic feudal contract whereby a vassal was required to serve his lord in the field for 40 days each year if required. The obligation to assist was equally binding on man and master, however. If the lord failed in his duty to protect his vassal, or to come to his relief when besieged, the vassal was considered to be in turn released from his obligations and was justified in suing for an independent peace.

Provisioning Any lord intending to garrison his castle and hold it against an attacker had first to consider the acquisition of supplies. Most castles had their own mills for grinding corn and at least one well. Salted meat and fish could be bought in and stored in bulk, and just before the attack cows, sheep and goats would be driven into the outer bailey or courtyard. From these milk (for cheese) and fresh meat could be obtained to augment the diet of salted flesh. The loss of the opportunity for hunting must have been sorely felt, since many medieval households relied on the chase for much of their meat.

The importance of the castle well can perhaps be gauged from a post-medieval example. In 1648 the Commonwealth forces attempted to seize Pembroke castle. They took the bailey, but could not take the keep. Eventually, the source of the water supplying the well in the keep was revealed through treachery. The Parliamentarians poisoned the water and the defenders of the keep surrendered—but not before they had discovered who had betrayed them, and dropped him down the well!

Perhaps for this sort of reason, beer and wine figure prominently in the royal accounts relating to the stocking of castles. More prosaically, such items as firewood, candles, charcoal and iron (for the repair and replacement of weapons), and timber and ropes for making catapults and other armaments, could make a vital contribution to the defence of the castle.

Garrisons The form of a castle reflected the level of manpower expected to be available for its defence. A Roman fort or a castle like Caernarvon presupposed the presence within its walls of a field army, whereas a

The square keep at Rochester, Kent, built *c.* 1127–40: a stark symbol of power and authority

motte and bailey was designed to be held by a relatively small number of men.

A medieval magnate travelled from place to place accompanied by his retinue, which included mounted knights. If he decided to put his castle into a state of defence, his knights were available for that defence. Should he have more than one castle, however, these men were not available for the defence of those other properties.

The standing garrison of a medieval castle was often quite small. Burton-in-Lonsdale, on a 'care and maintenance' basis in the 1130s, contained one knight, ten sergeants, a watchman and a porter—a garrison which cost £21 a year to maintain. More usually, a garrison in time of peace would house the constable and his family, together with a few domestic servants, a chaplain (who might also act as clerk and book-keeper), a smith or armourer, a watchman, a couple of sergeants and a dozen or so men-at-arms. Even at a larger castle like Conway, the standing garrison in 1284 comprised only the constable and his family, a chaplain, a mason, a smith, an armourer, a carpenter, 15 archers and 15 others including watchmen and servants. The garrison of Harlech was 37 men when it was betrayed to Owain Glyndwr for that 'sum of money', but it may have been under strength at the time. The major 'set piece' sieges, on the other hand, occurred where defenders had been concentrated in a single castle. Thus Rochester, at the time of the great siege of 1215, held 100 knights and men-at-arms. Dover, the same year, contained 140 knights, plus an unknown number of sergeants and men-at-arms—a small army, bottled up in the castle by the invading French.

Even in times of peace, the logistic arrangements for garrisoning a castle such as Dover could be quite complex. The eight major landowners owing 'castle guard' at Dover in the 12th century had each to provide a quota of knights for periods varying between 20 and 32 weeks each year. Since the number of knights whose service was due depended upon the number of smaller estates making up the main holding, and varied from five to twenty-five, the constable must have spent considerable time working out his guard rotas.

Because of complexities such as these there was an inevitable move to commuting the feudal duty of castle guard into a money payment, known as *scutage*. With the money so gained, professional men-at-arms and archers could be hired. Thus, at Dover in 1216, after the abortive siege by Prince Louis of France, it was decided that the old arrangements would have to be scrapped. In the words of the official report, 'every knight due for one month's guard duty should pay ten shillings, and henceforward both knights and foot-soldiers should be hired for guarding the castle'.

Professionalism of this sort must have eased the problem to some extent. Nevertheless, there was always the danger that a swift pre-emptive strike would carry a castle before it could be put into a state of defence, since few lords could afford to pay for large permanent garrisons all the year round. Thus it was possible in 1140 for Ranulf, Earl of Chester, to establish himself firmly in the Castle of Lincoln, having gained entry while ostensibly on a sociable Christmas visit.

The Effectiveness of Castles Earl Ranulf's successful coup raises the question of why such apparently impregnable fortresses changed hands so readily in time of war.

Firstly, it must be remembered that while a medieval magnate travelled almost incessantly from castle to castle within his domains, he could be physically present in only one of them at any one time. He was thus forced to rely on the loyalty of his constables for the safe holding of his other castles. Even where the owner was resi-

72

dent, he himself might have doubts as to where his loyalties lay; the political issues might be unclear, or his lord might have forfeited claim to his loyalty. It was not unreasonable for William the Lion, King of Scotland, invading England in 1173, to ask Roger de Stuteville, constable of the border Castle of Wark,

> 'how he would act:
> whether he would hold it or surrender:
> which course he would pursue?'

A cautious man, with a wish to stay alive, Roger asked for a 40-day truce, the intention being that if relief were not forthcoming within that time he would surrender the castle on terms. It is significant that the Scots accepted this, and moved on to attack Alnwick, possibly in the hope of taking at least that castle by surprise.

Surprise was always the most effective weapon. The sudden, if treacherous, acquisition of Lincoln by the Earl of Chester has been mentioned, and when war or rebellion broke out it was always something of a race to gather provisions and defenders on the one side, and siege engines and attackers on the other.

Few castles seem to have fallen by direct assault. The bailey gate could often be fired, or the curtain wall scaled, but the great keep was usually proof against assault. In the two great sieges fought to the bitter end— Rochester (1215) and Bedford (1224), it was mining that laid the keeps open to assault. The two methods of attack most likely to succeed in the long term were thus the mine and the blockade. Of these, the quicker was the mine, but even this relied to some extent on slow drawn out psychological effect. One never knew when a mine would be fired and one's defence (and home) demolished, and the waiting and the uncertainty must have been hard to endure.

The effect of being under siege is hard now to imagine, but the psychological pressures must have been great, exacerbated as they were by privation and disease. As weeks and even months went by and relief did not come, the garrison was forced to remain always upon the defensive. The initiative lay at all times with the attacker, and this fact in itself must have taken its toll of the defenders' morale. No doubt it was to retain the illusion of offensive action, as much as for any real gain, that sallies were undertaken.

In the last resort, a well-built castle could hold out for as long as the will to resist remained—or at least, for as long as the defenders thought it worthwhile to resist. War fought face to face is always more sparing of life than war fought by remote control, and the object of medieval wars was not to destroy life, but to gain control of land and of the wealth that came from the land. Castles had to be taken because they sheltered the knights who controlled the lands under dispute. A quick negotiated surrender was preferable from the point of view of both parties to a bitter, long drawn out blockade.

To end on a more personal note, we may listen to Jane Pelham, besieged at Pevensey in 1399 by adherents of Richard II, and writing solicitously to enquire after the health of her absent husband, a supporter of the future Henry IV.

'My dere Lorde, I recommende me to your hie Lordshippe with hert and body ... and thanke yhow, my dere Lorde, of your comfortable lettre that ye send me from Pownefraite that com to me on Mary Magdaleyn day; ffor by my trowth I was never so gladde as when I herd by your lettre that ye warr strong ynogh with the grace off God for to kepe yow fro the malyce of your ennemys ...

It is only at the end of the letter, and almost incidentally, that we hear of her own predicament.

... and my dere Lorde, if it is lyk yow for to know off my ffare, I am here by layd in manner off a sege with the

74

The 13th-century round keep at Tretower, Powys, standing within an earlier shell keep of the 12th century built to consolidate the Anglo-Norman hold on mid Wales

Counte of Sussex, Sudray and a greet parsyll off Kente, so
that I ne may nogth out, nor none vitayles gette me but
with myche hard. Wherefore, my dere, if it lyk yow by
the awyse off yowr wyse counsell, for to sett remadye off
the salvation off yhower castell ... Farewell my dere
Lorde, the Holy Trinyte yow kepe fro your ennemys, and
son send me gud tythyngs off yhow. Ywryten at Pevensey
in the castell, on Saynte Jacobe day last past, by yhowr
awnn pore

J Pelham'

The letter is addressed 'To my trew Lorde'.

V THE HOUSES IN THE CASTLE

The presence of Jane Pelham at Pevensey serves to remind us that the medieval castle played a domestic role as well as a military one, for (as already noted) a castle was essentially a fortified house—albeit a house built on a large scale.

Today the domestic role is often less apparent than the military one. While the curtain walls and towers may survive to bear witness to the threat of siege and the need for defence, the less massively constructed buildings known in medieval times as 'the houses in the castle' have frequently collapsed or been removed. Many castles played no great part in the military affairs of their day, remaining peaceful residences and the administrative centres of large estates. It is ironic that so much of what remains should relate in so many cases to such a small part of the castle's lifespan, the longer periods of peaceful use being represented only by tumbled foundations. Yet just as the shell of a crab may be found lying on a beach long after the organism it was designed to protect has rotted away, so the outer walls of a castle may remain long after the decay of its internal structures.

The primary function of the medieval castle was thus from the start a dual one. A base for mounted troops, it was also the private residence of the leader of those troops, and once the military situation had created the need for a castle, other elements of the social and political structure came to be centred on it. A castle was thus not only a military base and fortified house: it was also a centre of local government and justice, an armoury, a prison and a bank. It might also be a toll station or frontier post. Within the protective shell of its walls and towers, the castle builder had to make provision for all these activities, reconciling so far as was possible the virtually irreconcilable requirements of comfort and defence. The balance achieved varied from castle to castle at any one time, and from time to time within any one castle, according to the competence of the designer and the brief given him by his patron.

While a minor lord might possess only one castle and reside there all the time, a magnate travelled from castle to castle accompanied by his 'household'. This might be a large and complex affair comprising (in addition to his knights) his family and their domestic servants, his chaplain, his treasurer, several apprentice knights in the role of esquires, cooks, falconers, grooms and huntsmen—in all 50 people or more. The king and his major barons might be accompanied by much greater numbers. On reaching their destination all these required accommodation within the castle. Between such visits, on the other hand, the castle might be occupied by only the score or so of people who made up the permanent garrison. As society became more highly organized, and the desire for a greater degree of comfort came to be expressed at all levels, the castle builder was required by his patron to provide accommodation not only for the patron's own household, but also for the households of visiting lords. Gradually, during the 13th and 14th centuries, architectural skills increased and 'the houses in the castle', at first separate and scattered within the castle bailey, came to be integrated with the defensive shell itself; gatehouses carried suites of rooms in their upper storeys and wall towers acted as high-rise apartment blocks. Ultimately the domestic buildings became the castle, enclosing a courtyard defined by their inner walls, while their outer walls formed the curtain.

The Hall Over and above his need for a comfortable house, the medieval lord had a need for a large room in which he could discharge his public duties. This room was the hall. Contrary to popular belief, at high levels of society the hall was not the centre of domestic life, being reserved rather for the holding of courts and formal receptions. Thus the kitchen serving the hall was not necessarily that serving the apartments in which the lord lived with his family: hall, kitchen, buttery (where drinks were kept) and pantry (for dry goods) formed a unit brought into use only on special occasions. However, since such special occasions reflected—and could be made to emphasize—the lord's status in society, the hall and its attendant rooms usually formed the most eye-catching element within the castle's defences.

The most obvious example of this is the keep. In many cases the keep shows, arranged vertically, the same sequence of rooms as are to be found elsewhere arranged horizontally at ground level. By the 13th century, however, there was usually a separate great hall for formal purposes standing in the bailey. This might be one of two basic types, distinguished by the position of the hall, either raised above or placed at ground level. In its earlier and simpler form the hall was placed at first-floor level above a storage basement or undercroft. At one end was a small chamber entered from the hall itself and sometimes also from a separate stair. It was in this latter chamber that the lord lived with his family. In the more grandiose examples this chamber might be served by a latrine and have its own chapel. Sometimes the ground floor was used, not as a store, but to provide accommodation similar to that provided above at first-floor level: in such cases, the upper complex of hall and chamber was the more luxurious.

This 'doubling up' of halls indicates that provision was being made for the accommodation of more than

20, 108
163

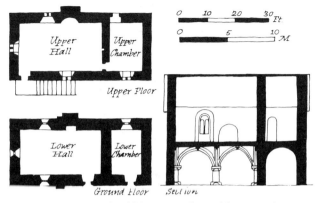

Plans and section of a 12th-century 'house' incorporating two superimposed halls, each with its own chamber

one household within the same castle. Usually the lower and less luxurious hall and chamber would have been used by the constable and his family, while the upper hall and chamber were reserved for the lord himself when in residence.

The larger keeps of the 12th century occasionally show the same arrangement, with suites of rooms placed one above the other, each forming a self-contained residence. Again, the lower, or lowest suite would have been used by the constable, since this suite had the easiest access and was thus appropriate for someone concerned with the day-to-day running of the castle. The upper suite (or suites), being more remote and hence more private, would then have served the lord, his family and his guests. This assumption, that on occasion several distinct households would occupy a single castle, each with a hall and chamber for its use, characterizes all medieval castle planning, though it is seen most dramatically in the great works of the 14th and 15th centuries.

80

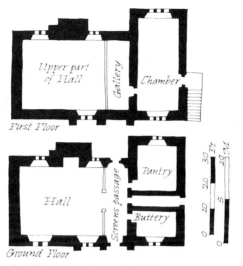

Plans of a 13th-century 'house' with single hall rising through two storeys and two-storey chamber/service wing

An alternative, and from the 13th century a more common form of disposition of hall and chamber was to place the hall at ground level, with its attendant chambers arranged in two storeys at one end. Frequently there was very limited access between the hall and the chambers, bearing out the contention that the hall was not regularly used by those occupying the chambers.

Where extra space was required, or the status of the owner demanded, the hall might be aisled. Doors were usually placed opposite each other in the side walls towards one end of the building and a screen was often erected so as to create a corridor across this end of the hall: this became known as the *screens passage*. From this passage there was access to the hall, at the far end of

24, 99
163

5, 24
109

which a dais might be placed to emphasize the dignity of the lord and his closest associates. Heating was provided by an open fire, often burning in the middle of the hall floor. With the fire in such a position there could be no chimney, and so the smoke escaped (or failed to escape) through a hole in the roof topped by a chimney pot or louvre. Later, in the 14th century, the fire was usually laid in a specially built fireplace, set at one side of the hall where it could be served by a chimney.

On the further side of the screens passage lay the 'service rooms', the pantry and buttery. Kitchens, for obvious reasons, constituted a fire risk and were usually built detached, but near the pantry and buttery. In the 14th century a second corridor was often contrived at right angles to the screens passage, running between the pantry and buttery to a door at the end of the building from which the separate kitchen could be quickly reached.

11, 72
163

The hall itself was open to the roof in a single tall storey (i.e., there was no ceiling). Above the service rooms, however, there was space for a second storey, and here could be placed the lord's chamber or chambers. Pantry and buttery could thus be made to serve the lord's chambers above on a daily basis and the more formal hall on special occasions. This complex of rooms at one end of the hall thus constituted a virtually independent house, to which the hall was attached, the various rooms functioning together in a variety of ways according to the importance of the occasion.

Domestic Planning So long as the domestic buildings of the castle were considered as separate entities, standing free within the bailey, it was possible for the layout described above to be followed fairly exactly, and it is where the constraints of military security were least felt that the plan was most logically set out. The form is thus not confined to castles, but may be found in un-defended manor houses and the houses of the gentry. Echoes of it can still be found in the great houses of the 16th century and in the lesser houses of the 17th century. Where the space available was limited by the terrain or by the dictates of the military architect, however, modifications had to be made. Then the hall might be built against the curtain wall and a convenient wall tower might be made to serve as a chamber block. As the overall plans of newly built castles became more geometric, and the desire for comfort increased, halls, chambers, kitchens and service rooms became ever more intricately disposed within the rigid frame dictated by the defensive elements of the castle.

This development did not occur suddenly, but was spread over a century or more. The requirement for separate residences—'the houses in the castle'—was of long standing, and the accommodation provided in response to it was still relatively loosely scattered in most 13th-century castles. Even within symmetrically conceived castles like Beaumaris and Harlech the domestic 86, 109 accommodation was simply tacked onto the defensive shell, overflowing into the gatehouse and wall towers, without any real integration of the twin requirements of domesticity and defence. During the 14th century, however, the increasing formalization of social life, to be seen in the creation of knightly orders of chivalry, resulted in a demand for quite elaborate and sophisticated layouts.

A good example is Bodiam in Sussex, built by Sir 11 Edward Dalyngrigge at the end of the 14th century. Sir Edward had done well out of the French wars earlier in the century, but now the tide of war had turned and his lands in Sussex were vulnerable to French raiders. In 1385 he received a licence to fortify his house 'with a wall of lime and mortar', these being the usual terms of a royal permit to build a private castle at this time.

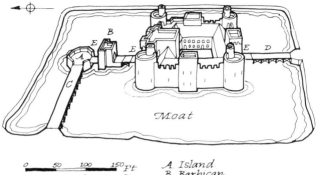

0 50 100 150 Ft	A. Island.
0 10 20 30 40 50 M	B. Barbican.
	C. Bridge.
	D. Bridge to Postern Gate.
	E. Drawbridges.

Bodiam, Sussex: Sir Edward Dalyngrigge's dream castle, set in its moat

The castle he built was almost square in plan, with round towers at the corners and square ones in the middle of the intervening walls. The whole was set round by a moat as a protection against mining.

Sir Edward evidently demanded that the new castle should incorporate at least seven separate halls. One was to be the Great Hall, reserved for ceremonial occasions: it was equipped with a screens passage and service rooms placed either side of a central passage running through to a kitchen beyond, with a great chamber above the service rooms. This complex, the symbol of Sir Edward's station in life, was placed on the main axis of the castle facing the visitor directly across the court-yard from the gateway. A second hall, at first-floor level in the neighbouring east wing, was apparently for Sir Edward's personal use, having an anteroom, three smaller inner chambers and a tiny private pew opening into the south side of the chapel. Below this suite was a third hall with two chambers opening off it. If the

84

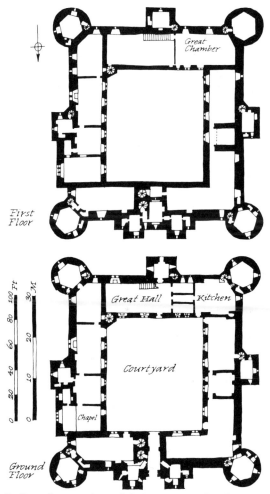

First
Floor

Great
Chamber

Great Hall

Kitchen

Courtyard

Chapel

Ground
Floor

100 Ft 80 60 40 20 0

30 M 20 10 0

Bodiam, Sussex: plans of the ground and first floors

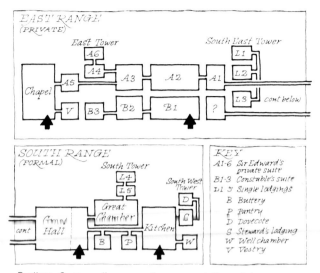

EAST RANGE
(PRIVATE)

East Tower

A6
A4
A5   A3   A2   A1

Chapel

V   B3   B2   B1   ?

South East Tower

L1
L2
L3   cont below

SOUTH RANGE
(FORMAL)

South Tower

L4
L5

Great
Chamber

Great
Hall

cont

B   P

Kitchen

South West
Tower

D
G
W

KEY
A1-6   Sir Edward's
          private suite
B1-3   Constable's suite
L1-5   Single lodgings
B   Buttery
P   Pantry
D   Dovecote
S   Steward's lodging
W   Well chamber
V   Vestry

Bodiam, Sussex: diagrammatic representation of the accommodation in the east and south ranges

12th-century usage was still retained, this lower suite would have been for the use of the constable. We thus find the lord of the castle ensconced in a fairly luxurious suite of six rooms at first and second-floor level, above a simpler constable's suite at ground level, with an elaborate arrangement of great hall, pantry, buttery and great chamber reserved for formal occasions.

Accommodation for guests of a status comparable with that of Sir Edward was provided in four further halls. In the east part of the north wing were two halls at ground-floor and first-floor levels, with chambers opening off them in the north-east tower. Similarly, two halls were built one above the other in the south part of the west wing, where there was another kitchen. Since the arrangements in the north-west angle of the castle cannot now be determined, there may have been

Part fantasy and part reality—Sir Edward Dalyngrigge's 'moated dream castle' at Bodiam in Sussex disguises a large and comfortable country house of the 1380s

even more accommodation than has already been listed.

These four suites of rooms were evidently for the simultaneous entertainment of up to four visiting magnates, each of whom might expect to arrive, and to be accommodated, with his own household about him. Even so, there would be others who were not so accompanied and for whom a single room would be sufficient, providing it was well heated and equipped with a private latrine. For such guests there were at least nine single-chamber lodgings placed in the various towers, plus two suites of three small rooms in the gatehouse. Some of these single lodgings, however, may normally have been occupied by the regular inhabitants of the castle. Thus the single lodging in the south-west tower may have been for the steward, who would need to supervise affairs in the nearby kitchen, buttery and pantry, while one of the lodgings near the chapel must have been used by the chaplain unless he slept in the vestry. It is possible also that one of the halls in the west range may have been for the use of the domestic staff rather than guests.

Where the cooks, scullions, grooms and stable-lads slept is far from clear. Possibly they were expected to sleep in the places where they worked. On great occasions, when all the guest accommodation was taken up, the corridors, kitchens, storerooms and stables must have been crowded with people looking for somewhere to lay their heads. Squires would have been expected to sleep together, and so would the maids, ladies-in-waiting and the like. For the latecomer, it must sometimes have been easier to put up at the local inn.

Furniture and Décor   A modern visitor, entering a medieval apartment, would probably be struck by the rather bare appearance of the room. At that time floors were covered by rush mats; carpets, when they were first imported from the East, were hung on the walls
88

like tapestries. Tapestries were the usual means of decorating walls, absorbing sound and generally softening the harsh contours of stonework. Alternatively, walls might be plastered and painted. In 1240 Henry III ordered the Queen's Chamber in the Tower of London to be panelled and whitewashed and painted with roses, a decoration that must have been a welcome relief from Henry's favourite design of gold stars on a green background. A panelled screen was to be built between the chamber and the latrine, and the latrine itself was to be tiled. For himself, he ordered that 'the chamber where the King washes his head' was to be painted with the story of the king who was saved by his dogs from the treachery of his subjects.

Such scenes were also wrought in stained glass. Chaucer, writing of John of Gaunt's first wife, describes the feeling of being woken by the song of birds in the early morning, and on looking around—

> '...sooth to seyn my chambre was
> Ful wel depeynted, and with glas
> Were al the windowes wel y-glased
> Ful clere, and not an hole y-crased,
> That to beholde hit was gret joye;
> For hoolly al the Storie of Troye
> Was in the glasyng y-wroght thus—
> Of Ector, and Kyng Priamus,
> Of Achilles, and of Lamedon,
> And eke of Medea and of Jasoun;
> Of Paris, Eleyne and of Lavyne—
> And al the walles with colours fyne
> Were peynted, both text and glose
> With all the Romance Of The Rose.'

Panelling, wall-hangings, painted plaster and coloured glass thus transformed bare stone chambers into apartments worthy of a queen or duchess. Poorer lords, however, might be able to aspire to only one or two hangings, or a more restricted scheme of painting, and in many castles the walls were simply whitewashed.

Furniture was scanty by modern standards. According to an inventory made in 1397 there were in the great hall of the house in question three trestle tables, one fixed table, two chairs, three benches and three stools. There were two cushions for the chairs, and two short lengths of tapestry to hang over their backs. There were also two brass wash-basins, two large pots, two pieces of crockery and three fire-irons. No other furniture is mentioned, though it is possible that some had been removed before the inventory was taken. We might have expected to hear of a cupboard and a chest or two for storing linen, drinking vessels and so forth. Apart from this, the inventory is fairly typical. Even the apartments of the rich, while they might be bright with colour, were sparsely furnished.

Such movable furniture was of course augmented by stone benches built into the arched embrasures of windows. These window seats allowed work such as sewing, embroidery, fine carving and the like to be carried out in good light and fresh air. In general, however, and particularly in winter, air and light were in short supply. Although by the later 14th century John of Gaunt's duchess might have glazed windows in her bedroom, glass was not common. Windows might be covered against draughts by movable screens of oiled linen, which if not transparent was at least translucent. Broadly speaking, it was possible to have warmth or natural light, but rarely both.

Bathrooms and Latrines   Henry III was unusual in having a separate chamber where he might 'wash his head'. For the most part, bathrooms as such are conspicuously lacking. Washing, when done at all, was done in large tubs close to the fire. King John took at least 12 baths in 1209. We know this from the royal accounts, which record the 4 pence paid on each occasion to the man who gathered wood and heated the water: by the end of the year, however, the price had gone up to 5 pence, about £15 in present-day terms. Bathing was thus not to be undertaken lightly. Even Edward, 2nd Duke of York and a grandson of Edward III, describing the joys of hunting at the end of the 14th century, seems to have regarded washing as one of the grim necessities of life. When the huntsman returns, we are told, 'he shall doff his clothes and his shoes and his hose, and he shall wash his thighs and his legs... and peradventure all his body'.

Latrines, on the other hand, were important items. The communal latrines of large monastic houses often vented into a stream culverted below the building, so that they were constantly flushed. Such refinements were not to be found in most castles. Small latrines, known as garderobes, were contrived in the thickness of the outer walls of buildings, or in specially built towers projecting from the main structure. Their open shafts vented into pits which were emptied from time to time, or into the castle ditch or moat. Latrines of this sort were thus limited to those parts of the castle where a vent was possible, and not everyone would have access to them. Chamber pots do not seem to have been used during the Middle Ages, and so a long walk to the communal latrine or 'jakes' in the bailey was necessary for many people. Perhaps the most remarkable latrines of all were those built at Conway in 1286 at a cost of £15 99 (in today's terms, perhaps some £4500). Close to the walls of the new town adjoining Edward I's great castle stood 'the king's wardrobe', the building housing his private secretariat. This was the administrative hub of the royal household. For the Keeper of the Wardrobe and his clerks a battery of no less than 12 latrines were built projecting over the battlements of the town walls. Why so many latrines were necessary, when other people had so few, is not clear. Perhaps a certain view of the Civil Service prevailed even then!

Prisons   As the seat of a royal sheriff or a major magnate enjoying rights of justice over the surrounding area, a castle might often serve as a prison. Some castles were regularly used in this way. Thus St Briavels, for example, was the administrative centre for the royal Forest of Dean: here were imprisoned those who infringed the laws of the Forest.

A castle might also house prisoners of noble birth. Charles d'Orléans spent many years in honourable captivity in the Tower of London after his capture at Agincourt in 1415, while James I of Scotland was interned at Windsor. For the most part prisoners of high rank were treated well. After all, the object of capturing them was usually to extort ransom, and who would pay for a dead prisoner? Only persons awaiting trial, or legally condemned to imprisonment, would be kept under lock and key.

Nevertheless, the modern visitor will be shown a 'dungeon' in almost every castle. Usually this will be a small, ill-lit, underground chamber. The use of the word dungeon for a prison is incorrect. 'Dungeon' is just a corruption of *donjon*, the medieval word for a keep, and reflects the fact that while keeps were designed to keep people out, they could also be used to keep people in. The ground-floor room of a keep, which could be entered only from above and which had narrow windows placed high up in the walls, could thus be used not only for storage but also for the confinement of prisoners if necessary. Cold and dark such rooms might be, but only because all storerooms were cold and dark. By no means all castles boasted a custom-built prison.

Where such prisons do exist they are rarely, if ever, underground. Often they are in the gatehouse, since there would always be guards on duty there no matter how empty the rest of the castle might be. Most Tower Houses had at least one small prison chamber, built

92

either in the thickness of the wall or above the springing of a vault, to bolster the owner's claim to be lord of the surrounding lands.

Kitchens and Stores The lowest storey of the keep, being cool and dark, was usually the place for the bulk storage of beer, wine, salted meat and fish, and flour. Other foodstuffs, probably fairly quickly consumed, required little in the way of long-term storage. When visitors were expected, of course, huge quantities of food might be required. When King John spent Christmas at Winchester in 1206, the Sheriff of Hampshire was instructed to lay in 1500 chickens, 5000 eggs, 20 oxen, 100 pigs and 100 sheep!

For great occasions like this the large kitchens adjoining the great hall would be brought into service. Huge fireplaces with ovens built into their walls allowed the roasting of meat on spits, the baking of bread and the simmering of stews to be carried on simultaneously. On less formal occasions, when only a score or so of people might be present in the castle, there was little point in kindling such fires. Then cooking was probably done in smaller rooms over braziers. The 15th-century household book of the wealthy Percy family records that breakfast 'for my lord and lady' might consist of 'a loaf of bread in trenchers' (i.e., in slices), 'a quart of beer or wine, and two pieces of salt fish, herring or sprats'. Such meals needed no special rooms set aside for their preparation, though occasionally a small kitchen or servery can still be detected by the survival of a sink or drain for slops.

Water was drawn from wells, of which a large castle might have several. The vital importance of ensuring a good supply of water is shown by the effort which often went into the making of wells. In a motte and bailey castle the well-shaft was sometimes built upwards from ground level as well as dug downwards, so that

11, 46
89, 113
126, 133

23, 58

it rose like a chimney through the motte itself, enabling water to be drawn to a windlass on top of the motte. Where castles were set on rocky outcrops, the wells might have to be dug through solid rock to a depth of 60 m (200 ft) or more. In the case of a very deep well, the weight of the long rope, added to the weight of the water in the bucket, might be more than a man could manage, even with the aid of a windlass: in such cases
16 a treadmill might be used, worked by a donkey or mule.

Nearly always there was a separate well in the keep.
15, 68 Again, as with some mottes, the well shaft was built up through the walls of the keep so that water could
27 be drawn off at each floor. At Dover, water was drawn to the well-head at second-floor level and there tipped into a cistern: from this lead pipes built into the walls distributed the water to taps in the various rooms—an unusually lavish system, fully in keeping with general standards in this, the greatest of Henry II's keeps.

Colleges and Chapels   Every castle boasted at least
46, 59 one chapel. This might be a free-standing building in
66, 86 the bailey, or it might be contrived in one of the wall towers or in a chamber adjoining the hall. Where there
13, 29 was a keep, however, there was always a separate chapel
58, 80 within it for the use of the lord of the castle when he resided there. Often the chapel occupied the upper part of the 'forebuilding' which protected the entrance to the keep. That this was not just a matter of convenience is suggested by the way in which chapels were also built in the upper parts of gatehouses protecting the entrances of walled towns. A common dedication was to St Michael, a warrior saint, whose aid might be invoked when the castle came under attack. Where the keep offered accommodation for constable and lord on separate floors, each apartment might be provided with
27, 68 a chapel in which the sumptuousness of the carving varied in accordance with the status of the user. These
94

small chapels were thus private ones, meeting the needs of a single household or a single family.

Where such private chapels existed there were also more public ones for the use of others in the castle. A few churches now used parochially were in origin castle chapels; these stand not in the centre of a village, but in the bailey of a now deserted castle.

The founding of a church or chapel was an act of piety, and some of the richer lords went so far as to establish within their castles chapels served by whole colleges of priests. The best known is probably the Chapel of St George which stands in the outer bailey of the royal castle of Windsor. Here, in 1240, Henry 84 III established a college of seven chaplains to serve his new chapel. A century later, Edward III rebuilt this chapel, increased the number of priests to 26 and added 26 'poor knights' who (in return for their food and shelter) were required to attend mass and pray for the souls of the King and the Prince of Wales and of the 24 newly created knights of the Order of the Garter. Only the west end of Edward's chapel survives: the present Chapel of St George was built at the end of the 15th century.

Almost as grandiose was the scheme planned by the Percy Earls of Northumberland at Warkworth. Devised 82 by the 1st Earl at the end of the 14th century and put into effect by the 2nd Earl in the middle of the 15th century, the idea was for a college of secular canons to be established in the bailey. A huge church was begun, blocking the whole northern end of the bailey: but the scheme was too grandiose for even the Percys' finances, and the building was never completed. More practical schemes were carried out elsewhere, however, the buildings of the new college being erected sometimes within the bailey and sometimes outside it. 76

Gardens Surrounding the castle, or tucked away in

95

odd corners of the bailey, were gardens and 'plea-
saunces'. Herb gardens were planted not merely for
pleasure: the herbs grown were used for cooking and
for preparing medicines and potions. For these reasons
99 the herb garden in the eastern barbican at Conway was
planted at a very early stage in the building of the castle.
The castle was hardly begun before March 1283, yet
already by July of the same year turf for the Queen's
lawn had been shipped up river to the castle, the garden
plot had been fenced round with staves from empty
wine barrels, and an esquire, Roger de Fykeys, was
being paid three pence to water the newly planted
garden. There were gardens in both the upper and
lower baileys at Windsor, and Henry II ordered a
garden to be made before the window of his chamber
at Arundel, which was in his hands at the time. Vine-
yards, too, were a source of pleasure, as were dovecotes.

External Appearance   Because a castle was as much
a home as a device of war, its owner was likely to take
pride in its appearance as well as in its strength. That
this was the case is borne out by a number of medieval
descriptions of castles which lay emphasis on the impression made by the combination of walls and towers,
the play of light and shadow on the stonework, and the
sounds of domestic life.

One factor affecting the appearance of a castle was
the whitewashing of its walls. Little evidence for this
99, 142 survives now on the walls themselves, but faint traces
can occasionally be seen in places sheltered from the
weather. However, the accounts kept by the constables
of royal castles often refer to sums of money spent on
whitening the external walls; the great keep of the
Tower of London, for instance, was regularly whitewashed during the medieval period—hence its name,
the White Tower. Such treatment of the walls would
help preserve them, but it would also have the effect

The arrogant panoply of late medieval life is made plain at Raglan in Gwent, built in the 1460s to mark Sir William Herbert's meteoric rise to power under the House of York (Reconstruction by Alan Sorrell)

of making a castle stand out more sharply against its background, increasing its domination of the landscape.

A second factor, the effect of which is more difficult to judge, was the form of the roofs—and especially the roofs of the towers. The miniature paintings of castles to be found in medieval French manuscripts show gleaming white castles with towers capped with conical roofs like witches' hats. Only one such roof of medieval date survives in France, and none in Britain, so it is difficult to be certain how prevalent this form of roof really was. Many castles 'restored' in the last century were 94 given conical roofs to their towers, and Castell Coch shows the two types of roof then thought to be characteristically medieval. One covers the entire top of the tower, the 'brim' of the hat-like roof covering the battlements and converting them into unglazed windows. The second type is contained within and behind the battlements, so that an open wall-walk is left between the slope of the roof and the battlements themselves.

No positive evidence of medieval date survives for either type in any British or Irish castle. At Caernar-
88, 99 von, and Conway, however, it is clear that if the towers were ever capped by conical roofs, those roofs did not cover the battlements, since these were provided with small finials or pinnacles which were evidently intended to stand free and to be seen. It is unfortunate that more than this cannot be said, since a castle provided with conical roofs on its whitewashed towers would have presented an appearance very different from that presented today.

It may be fitting to close this chapter with the words of two medieval writers, the one Welsh, the other French. Geraldus Cambrensis was immensely proud of
116 his family home, Manorbier Castle in south-west Wales. When Gerald wrote in the 12th century Manorbier was quite strongly defended, but his pride lay in

98

its homeliness as much as in its martial appearance—

> 'The castle called Maenor Pyrr is distant about three miles from Pembroke. It is excellently well defended by turrets and bulwarks, and is situated on the summit of a hill extending on the western side towards the seaport, having under its walls to the north and northwest an excellent fishpond, as conspicuous for its grand appearance as for the depth of its waters, and a beautiful orchard on the same side, enclosed on one part by a vineyard, and on the other by a wood, remarkable for the projection of its rocks and the height of its hazel trees. On the right hand of the promontory, between the castle and the church, near the site of a very large lake and mill, a rivulet of never-failing water flows through a valley, rendered sandy by the violence of the winds. Towards the west the Severn sea, bending its course towards Ireland, enters a hollow bay at some distance from the castle.'

The 13th-century French writer, Jean de Joinville, was equally fond of his family home. Leaving his castle to join Louis IX's Crusade, he tells us,

> 'I dared not look back towards Joinville, for fear lest my courage fail on leaving my two fine children and my fair castle of Joinville—which I loved in my heart.'

VI THE ELEMENTS OF THE CASTLE

In the preceding chapters an attempt has been made to answer such questions as 'Who built castles? How much did they cost? Why did they cease to be necessary?' The castle has been considered both as a device of war and as a home, and the main developments in military building from the 11th to the 15th centuries have been traced. The purpose of this chapter is to help the reader to recognize the different types of building which together make up a castle, and also to predict some of the features a visitor may expect to find inside those buildings.

EARTHWORK CASTLES

Castles of earth and timber require the greatest effort of imagination on the part of the visitor, for they have suffered the most at the hands of time. Much of their detail can be discovered only by archaeological excavation and is not apparent at first sight.

1, 30
57, 74
Ringworks These represent the earliest and simplest form of a castle. The domestic buildings of the lord's residence were encircled by a rampart and ditch, both of which will usually survive, though often in a highly eroded state. Norman ringworks in such a state are difficult to distinguish from the works of earlier ages, especially in Ireland where similar earthworks protected the houses of the pre-Norman chiefs. Often it is only the strength of their defences that marks them out. To qualify as a 'castle' in the later 11th century the lord's house had to be protected by a ditch at least 3 m (*c.* 10 ft) deep: if the spoil from such a ditch was piled along the

100

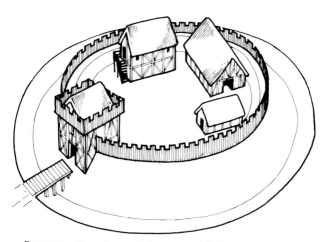

Reconstruction of a small ringwork with timber gatehouse and domestic buildings

inner edge to form a rampart, the combined obstacle would have been 6 m (*c.* 20 ft) high, with a timber breastwork adding a further 2 m (6–7 ft). In some cases, and perhaps in most, the earthen rampart was encased in timber to form an earth and timber wall. The evidence for this use of timber remains, after the timber had decayed and the earth has slumped, in the form of stains in the soil that can be revealed only by archaeological excavation. The casual visitor must use his imagination to restore the wooden walls topped with battlements.

The entrance through the defences was protected by a gatehouse. Traces of wooden gatehouses have been found by archaeologists, and from the few stone examples still standing we may envisage wooden 30, 64 towers at least 5 m (*c.* 16 ft) square in plan and standing 8 m (26 ft) or more in height: in some of the larger ringworks the gate towers may have been as much as

10 m (*c.* 33 ft) square and 15 m (*c.* 50 ft) high. From the room above the entrance passage a portcullis could be worked. The drawbridge at this stage was probably just a removable section of a wooden bridge over the ditch.

This system of defence could enclose a courtyard large or small, according to the requirements of the owner. Some ringworks protected the manor houses of relatively impecunious lords, and were correspondingly small in diameter—perhaps some 40 m (*c.* 130 ft) across: others were royal castles and were considerably larger. Within the defences the basic requirements were a hall and chamber for the lord's use, a kitchen and a well, a stable, a workshop and perhaps a chapel. Other buildings, such as barns, might stand outside the defences. Sometimes a second 'ringwork' served as a bailey to the first

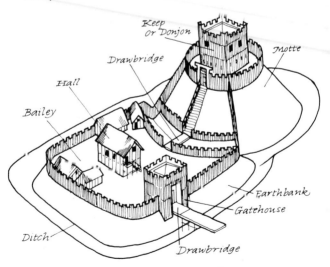

Reconstruction of a motte and bailey castle

As the simplest form of castle, ringworks continued to be built for several centuries, gradually sliding down the scale of importance as new methods of defence were perfected. The earliest Norman ringworks were built at the time of the Conquest, when the type could qualify as a royal castle: by the 13th century ringworks were being built only by minor lords whose resources could not rise to anything more sophisticated.

Motte and Bailey Castles

The motte and bailey castle is one of the distinguishing marks of early Norman military activity. The **motte,** a conical mound, may be made of piled earth or rock derived from an encircling ditch, or by scarping the sides of a convenient knoll. The ditch was essentially a quarry providing materials for the mound: although it might become flooded in wet weather, it was in no way a moat, and many mottes were surrounded by dry ditches. Some mottes were huge, reaching a height of 20 m (c. 65 ft). 77 Most, however, were much smaller, piled to a height of 5 m (c. 16 ft) or so above the underlying ground surface. The area of the summit, largely for practical reasons, tends to vary inversely with the height of the mound. Thus, the lower mottes often have room on top for a large building, whereas the taller mottes could have carried only a small tower. Very occasionally there is more than one motte in a castle, an arrangement of 43, 44 which the exact significance is not known; it may be that the lordship of such castles was shared in some way, each lord having his own motte. Such instances are rare, however, since the construction of a motte was a lengthy business involving months of work rather than days.

Accommodation on a motte, whatever its size, was bound to be limited. Most of the domestic buildings of the castle were, therefore, built at ground level nearby, within a **bailey** defended by a rampart and ditch. Often the defences of the bailey have been obliterated or hidden by modern buildings. Occasionally, however, it would seem that there was never a bailey, and hence never a proper residence. In such cases the motte was probably the symbol of an absentee lord, a place where his bailiff might hold court or receive rents on his behalf. Some of the more important castles boasted two or more baileys, but whether this represented a change of plan or a deliberate division between 'private' and 'public' areas is not clear.

The bailey was often kidney-shaped in plan, so that all parts of it were within bowshot from the motte. However, the shape of the terrain frequently dictated other plans and we find triangular, square and oblong baileys as well. Where the earthworks of some earlier age were being adopted, they would impose their own constraints on the choice of a plan. Probably there was no ideal plan, each lord devising his own on the basis of past experience.

The ramparts were sometimes encased in timber, like the ramparts of some ringworks, and it may be that the intention with earthwork castles was always to form a wall of some sort, even if only of earth and timber. More dramatically, it would appear that some mottes were similarly encased in timber. In such cases no earth was visible at all, the castle apparently being made entirely of timber. Behind the scenes, however, the timber frame was filled with earth as a protection against battering rams.

On top of the motte there was usually a palisade and a tower. In some cases this tower was merely a strongpoint for archers. Ensconced in such a tower on top of a high motte a few crossbowmen could command the bailey and hold out against everything except fire and starvation. Some mottes, however, carried more grandiose buildings. Indeed, it is possible that the motte and the tower on its summit were to some extent regarded

104

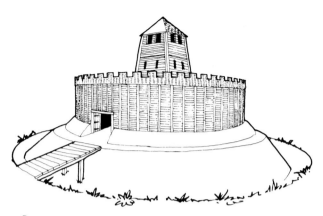

Reconstruction of the motte at South Mimms, Hertfordshire

as a single entity. This might be expressed structurally by burying the lower part of a tall tower in the mound so that the two were built up together, the mound buttressing the tower and acting as a fireproof plinth. At South Mimms in Hertfordshire archaeological excavation has shown that in the 12th century the motte (now a grass-grown mound) supported a timber tower at least 20 m (65 ft) tall, the lower part of which was buried in the earth mound. The mound itself was encased in timber, while the tower was plastered and painted. The result was an integrated structure having some of the characteristics of a keep. This could not have been guessed without excavation, the present shape of the motte giving no clue as to its former appearance.

Not all mottes were necessarily so constructed, but that the buildings they supported might be veritable keeps is clear from a number of contemporary descriptions. In Flanders, Arnold of Ardres built upon his motte in 1117 a timber house which was 'a marvellous example of the carpenter's craft . . . he created an almost

31, 44
79

105

impenetrable labyrinth, piling storeroom upon storeroom, chamber upon chamber . . . extending the larders and granaries into the cellars and building the chapel in a convenient place overlooking all else from high up on the eastern side'. There were, apparently, three storeys in this tower. On the ground floor were the storerooms, on the first the main living accommodation and kitchen, and on the second the bedrooms. Such towers, plastered and brightly painted, and hung with banners on special occasions, must have created quite a spectacle looming over the roofs of the peasants' houses.

Of the buildings in the baileys of earthwork castles, less is known, though archaeology is beginning to reveal some traces. Most seem to have possessed a hall for formal use, a kitchen, a forge and armoury, stables and barns—in short, much the same facilities as occurred in a ringwork. Indeed, the motte and bailey castle was in effect a ringwork to which a motte had been added.

Access to the motte was deliberately not made easy. The Bayeux Tapestry shows 'flying' bridges springing from the edge of the motte ditch and rising on pillars to reach the summit of the motte. Traces of such bridges have been found by excavation. Other mottes were scaled by steps cut in their sides. At South Mimms there was a tunnel through the lower part of the timber-sheathed motte into the basement of the tower: a similar method of entry may have been used in other castles of this sort.

The earliest mottes were built within two or three years of the Conquest. By the end of the 11th century most castles boasted a motte, though some early ring-works and stone castles were never so equipped. Mottes continued to be built in England as late as the 1170s, and the type was used well into the 13th century in Ireland, where there was a renewed demand for castles that could be built relatively quickly and cheaply to consolidate newly won territory.

KEEPS

Shell Keeps   In its simplest form the shell keep results from the rebuilding in stone of the timber palisade round the summit of a motte. Its diameter is thus controlled by that of the motte, and may vary from 15 to 45 m (*c.* 50 to 150 ft). In alternative form the wall is built up from the base of the motte, encasing it in stone: this represents a translation into stone of timber revetments of the South Mimms type.

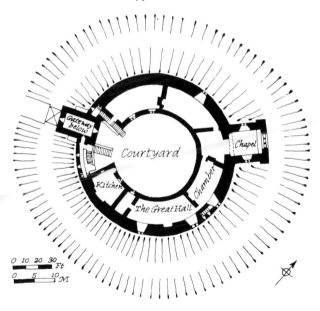

Restormel, Cornwall: an 11th-century ringwork converted to a shell keep

In plan the shell keep may be circular, oval or polygonal, in this again echoing the shape of the motte. The walls may rise from 6 to 10 m (*c.* 20 to 33 ft) in height. The masonry is rarely of fine quality, the stones being usually uncoursed and often undressed. Sometimes the stones are set diagonally, at 45°, alternate courses sloping different ways to give a 'herring bone' effect. Occasionally evidence may survive for a timber lacing within the wall, designed to spread the weight of the stonework and prevent cracking. Only in a few instances do battlements survive, but it is likely that the tops of most shell keeps were battlemented originally.

The entrance to a shell keep is usually just a simple doorway in the wall. Rarely, there may be a small tower commanding the entrance. Wall towers projecting from the shell wall can also be found on occasion, and may once have been more common.

Within the shell wall the interior buildings have usually disappeared, though later medieval structures may preserve an echo of original timber buildings grouped against the shell, leaving an open courtyard in the centre. At Restormel in Cornwall the 'shell keep' is really a glorified ringwork, being set at ground level: but here in the 13th century the internal buildings were rebuilt in stone and survive, so that we can see, arranged on two storeys round an open courtyard, features such as the hall, kitchen, chamber, chapel and storerooms, that are missing in other examples.

Shell keeps were built to replace wooden palisades on mottes within a generation of the Conquest. How long they continued to be built is less clear, but some examples may date from the later 12th or even the early 13th centuries.

Square Keeps   At its simplest, the square keep takes the form of a stone hall raised to first-floor level and entered at this level from an external flight of wooden

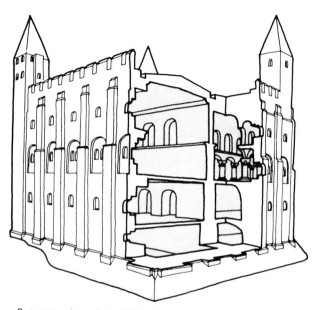

Cut-away view of the White Tower in the Tower of London, built c. 1088–1100

or stone steps. Built on a sufficiently large scale, and with its thickened walls penetrated at ground level only by slit windows, such a hall could function as a keep.

By placing a large chamber adjacent and parallel to the hall a more compact plan was achieved, resulting in a building almost square in plan and two storeys in height. Such early **hall keeps** are fairly plain on the outside, the main mass of the building being enriched by pilaster buttresses and broken only by the projecting apse of a chapel. Spiral stairs are placed in the corners, running from the entrance floor (i.e., first-floor level) downwards to the ground-floor basement, and upwards to the battlements. In one case the accommodation is doubled, giving two storeys above the basement.

22, 80
1 Until recently, only two such early 'hall keeps' were known. A third has now been discovered by excavation. On such restricted evidence it is impossible to generalize about details. During the 12th century, 54, 67 however, two further lavishly decorated hall keeps were built, continuing the idea of a large house of two (or, at the most three) storeys, with its entrance at first-floor level and its ground-floor windows kept narrow as a security measure. Again, however, it is difficult to generalize about these buildings.

About the same time, however, the **tower keep** was being evolved. This covers a smaller area of ground (usually 20–25 m or 65–82 ft square), but is taller, rising through three or four storeys to a height of 30–35 m (98–115 ft). As with the earlier 'hall keeps', the external 24, 34
52 walls are decorated (rather than buttressed) by pilaster strips rising from a splayed plinth. The plinth not only spread the load of the walls, but provided additional protection at ground level against attack by battering ram. Missiles dropped from the battlements would also ricochet off the sloping plinth in a disconcerting and dangerous fashion. The corners of the tower may be strengthened by closely placed pilasters or buttresses, or 27, 38
156 they may be encased within square corner turrets which rise above the main roof level.

The roofs are generally of very low pitch, almost flat in fact. A square keep would need two parallel roofs, since timbers to span more than 10 m (c. 33 ft) could not easily be found. The outer faces of the walls are carried up above the level of the roof to protect it against fire arrows and to serve as a parapet. This may be battle- 67, 142 mented, and may also have sockets for timbers to carry a hourd. (Care must be taken to distinguish such sockets from simple drainage holes, and from the 'putlog holes' resulting from the removal of timber scaffolding used in the construction of the keep: these last form a regular

Castle Hedingham: a square keep of the mid 12th century

pattern up the walls of the keep from plinth to wall head.)

Windows are tall and narrow where they open through the outer face of the wall, especially at ground and first-floor levels. Not every tall narrow opening was an arrow-loop. Where the sides of the opening splay gently towards the interior of the building, the opening is best interpreted as a window designed to admit the maximum amount of light consistent with

111

keeping the exterior opening small enough to prevent unauthorized entry. For an archer to be able to use his bow effectively, an embrasure for him to stand in had to be hollowed out of the inner face of the wall.

Entry is almost always at first-floor level, approached by a stair against the outer side of the keep. Occasionally the stair may rise to the second storey so as to prolong the ascent and allow extra defensive measures to be taken. Either way, the stair is usually encased in a 'forebuilding' projecting from the side of the keep. The entrance to the forebuilding is protected by a door and portcullis, and further doors and portcullises may be added within it. A further refinement is the interruption of the stair by a pit crossed by a drawbridge. The sites of these drawbridges can often be detected even when the bridge has gone. The portcullises slid up and down in grooves cut in the stonework on either side of the entrance: a few stones with this characteristic groove cut in them usually survive to show where the portcullis once worked. All important doors, such as the door of the keep itself, would be locked by wooden bars sliding back and forth along a socket cut in the door jamb just behind the door itself. On one side the socket will be deep enough to accommodate the whole length of the bar when withdrawn: on the other jamb will be a socket just big enough to take the end of the bar when slid across behind the door.

From the top of the stair within the forebuilding the visitor enters the main body of the keep. This entrance floor forms the main public hall of the building, and may sometimes be entered through a small lobby. In the larger keeps this floor and the basement beneath may be divided by a cross-wall. This may be solid, or opened up by arches to form an arcade. Sometimes a well-shaft is built within the thickness of the cross-wall. A common pattern of access is for it to be necessary to cross the hall to reach an internal stair leading to the

112

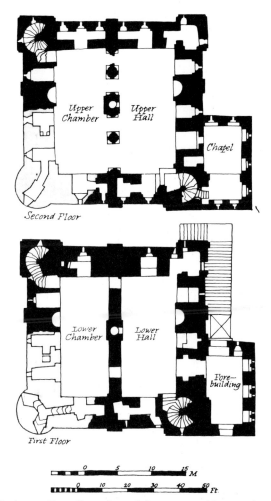

Upper Chamber

Upper Hall

Chapel

Second Floor

Lower Chamber

Lower Hall

Fore—building

First Floor

0   5   10   15 M

0   10   20   30   40   50 Ft.

Rochester, Kent: floor plans of the upper and lower suites in the keep

other floors. The stair will lead down to the ground-floor basement, which may occasionally be vaulted for 156, 184 extra strength and as a protection against fire, and upwards to the main residential floor above.

Where there is a cross-wall, this will usually be opened up by arches at the upper level. The rooms on this floor may be twice the height of those below, with narrow passages running in the thickness of the outer walls at two levels, the upper one reached by a stair and 27, 36 forming a gallery looking into the upper part of the 52 room. These passages lead to small rooms, which may have been private bedchambers, or to latrines. The 27, 68 windows in this upper floor will be larger than in the 36, 52 lower floors, and may be provided with window seats built into the jambs. Heating was by fires set in fireplaces, the flues rising in the thickness of the walls to the level of the roof. Kitchens can sometimes be distinguished, but large and elaborate kitchens were confined to the bailey. The upper part of the forebuilding, which is entered from this floor, may contain a chapel. 27, 190 Sometimes there will be more than one chapel in the 68 keep, each serving a different floor and hence a different household.

Square keeps were built throughout the 12th and 13th centuries. The last one to be built on any great scale in England was Dover, a work of the 1180s. However, smaller versions were built in the 13th century in Eng-180 land by lesser barons, and Greencastle (County Down)—a royal work of the mid 13th century—has a large rectangular keep. In Ireland in particular it is often difficult to draw a line between the smaller square keeps of the 13th century and the tower houses of the 14th and 15th centuries.

Round and Polygonal Keeps   There would seem to be no significant difference between keeps built in the round and those built from a polygonal ground plan.
114

Henry II's 'experimental' keep at Orford, Suffolk

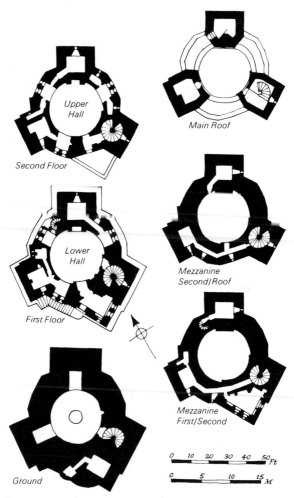

Second Floor

Upper Hall

Main Roof

First Floor

Lower Hall

Mezzanine
Second/Roof

Mezzanine
First/Second

Ground

0 10 20 30 40 50 Ft

0 5 10 15 M

Orford, Suffolk: an elaborate exercise in domestic planning

Most keeps of either sort show much the same interior layout as square keeps, with which they overlap in time.

The diameter may vary from 10 to 20 m (*c.* 33 to 66 ft) and the height from 15 to 25 m (*c.* 50 to 80 ft). Those towers built from a circular ground plan present the plainest exterior, being cylindrical in form and undecorated in any way. Some polygonal keeps have pilaster buttresses, resembling those found on square keeps, running up the angles. Most remarkable of all are those so-called 'transitional' or 'experimental' types, where large rectangular turrets project from the wall of the keep after the fashion of square keeps such as Dover. Smaller semicircular turrets continue the idea, and the two together produce some remarkable multi-lobed plans in the mid 13th century. The form of the roofs is not known, but they are likely to have been conical in shape and low pitched. One keep retains a stone vault to its top storey, and it may be that other keeps once had the same, though no evidence for this survives.

Entry is at first-floor level, as in most square keeps. Occasionally there is a forebuilding, but such buildings were difficult to adapt to the circular form, and a simple stair—perhaps interrupted by a drawbridge—is more common. The sequence of rooms is as in the square keep. There is a basement at ground level, entered only from above and lit (if at all) by a few narrow windows. The entrance floor is the public hall and is better lit. The cylindrical form does not lend itself to elaborate internal planning, and so the upper floors tend to repeat the arrangements of the entrance floor. Usually the arrangement of the stair is simpler than in the square keep, a single spiral in the thickness of the wall leading from basement to battlements. Floors are of timber, although occasionally the basement may be vaulted. The upper rooms are equipped with fireplaces, windows (sometimes with window seats) and latrines

18, 56
78

23, 58

45

62, 70
85

120

18, 58

23, 120
141

23, 185
45, 103

117

similar to those found in square keeps. No kitchens can be identified other than at Orford, though small sinks can sometimes be found. Identifiable chapels occur only at Conisburgh and Orford, and here both are accommodated within the main body of the keep. Only at Orford is there an upper gallery in the thickness of the wall, such as can sometimes be found in the upper hall level of square keeps. Indeed, by making full use of its forebuilding and three projecting turrets, Orford achieved a sophistication of domestic planning unequalled in any other round or polygonal keep.

No clear chronological succession can be seen in the building of round or polygonal keeps. The earliest non-rectangular keep (New Buckenham, a work of the 1150s) is round in plan: Henry II's Orford, a decade later, has projecting turrets. Pembroke, c. 1200, is round in plan, yet a few years later King John built an octagonal keep at Odiham. As with the square keep, the type lingered on, occurring as late as the 1270s at Flint and being revived in the mid 15th century at Raglan.

Tower Houses and Peels In Ireland and Scotland the peel or tower house is the poor man's keep, a compromise between comfort and security where the sudden raid is feared more than the prolonged siege. It is distinguishable from the square keep only by its smaller size and simpler build: in some cases no clear line can be drawn between the two.

The basic type is a tower of square or rectangular plan rising through three or more storeys, with a single room on each storey. The tower may be anything from 10 to 25 m (c. 33 to 80 ft) square in plan, and rise from 15 to 25 m (c. 50 to 80 ft) in height depending upon the number of storeys. The walls rise straight from the ground, or from a very small plinth: the great splayed plinth of the Norman keep is not found. The walls are unbroken by any projection, having no pilasters, but-

Section through the 15th-century tower house at Clara,
County Kilkenny

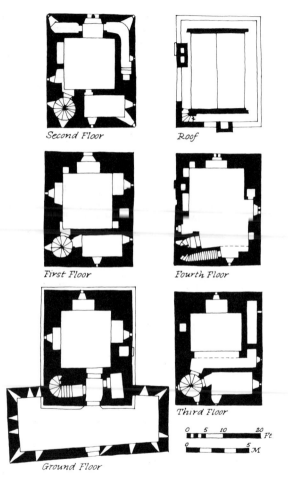

Second Floor

Roof

First Floor

Fourth Floor

Ground Floor

Third Floor

0   5   10   20 Ft

0   5 M

The tower house at Clara, Kilkenny: floor plans

tresses or turrets below the level of the parapet. The roof is usually fairly steeply pitched, unlike that of the earlier keeps, with stone gables. Timber hourds were carried on beams supported by a row of stone corbels projecting from the wall just below the parapet. By the early 15th century these hourds gave way to continuous stone machicolations, carried on stone corbels of ever-increasing elaboration. Indeed, the builders seem often to have compensated for the plainness of the walls by concentrating all the martial elements of the castle at roof level. Where there is no continuous machicolation around the top of the tower, there may be a small box-like machicolation above the door itself.

126, 139 169

Privacy is achieved not by subdividing the rooms on each floor, as in the Norman keep, but by adding extra wings (in Scotland known as 'jambs'), a single wing producing an L-shaped plan and two wings a U-shaped plan. More rarely, square corner turrets may be added. In 16th-century Scotland another variation was achieved by offsetting the wings to form a Z-plan. At the same time the roof was carried forward to rest on the oversailing parapets of the walls and small round turrets were built out on corbels from the square corners of the tower: occasionally the reverse occurs—square rooms being built out on corbels above round towers. The result is a profusion of conical roofs, gables and machicolations giving a very distinctive silhouette. In the 17th century Scottish settlers took the idea of this type of castle with them to Northern Ireland.

126, 130 170, 178

129

162

The entrance is usually at first-floor level. There is no forebuilding, the door being reached by a movable stair. The ground floor served as a basement for storage and is usually vaulted, a feature uncommon (though not unknown) in Norman keeps. It is lit only by narrow windows, as a security measure. Communication between this basement and the floor above is by trapdoor and ladder. From first-floor level upwards,

169, 176 178

communication is by means of a spiral stair in the thickness of the wall at one corner of the tower. Intermediary floors are of wood, but there is often a second vault over the top storey. The top and bottom of what is essentially a single house stood on end are thus protected against fire by stone vaults.

In a large tower house of more than three storeys, the storey above the basement may contain a kitchen. Alternatively, if the tower is provided with a wing or 'jamb', the kitchen will be in it, often equipped with a well, a sink and a fireplace. Either on the entrance floor, or on the floor above, is the hall. In the early examples, where the tower is square or rectangular in plan, the hall is simply a large room equipped with a fireplace in the gable wall, good sized windows and window seats. In later examples, where the tower has a wing or wings, one wing may house a chamber and the hall may have a screens passage at one end. Borthwick, in particular, by use of its two projecting wings, manages to achieve the full medieval layout of kitchen, screens passage, hall, chamber and latrine on a single floor, but this is not common. More usually, the chamber is above the hall and repeats its plan, with fireplace, windows with window seats, and perhaps a tiny oratory or chapel.

Whereas the 12th-century keep was the strongpoint of the castle, the tower house was itself the castle. Around it there is usually a small walled yard (a 'barmkin' in Scotland, a 'bawn' in Ireland). This is the ultimate reduction of the bailey, the yard being intended to house not men-at arms but sheep and cattle. The yard may be battlemented and provided with loops for either bows or hand-guns, and there may even be small corner towers, but it is clear that prolonged defence of the yard was never seriously contemplated.

The earliest tower houses date from the end of the 13th century, being derived from the small square keeps

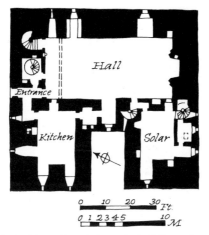

Borthwick, Lothian: plan of the main hall floor of a 15th-century tower house with two 'jambs'

still being built by those lords who could not afford a castle complete with wall towers, gatehouse and barbican. The basic idea—that of a fairly complete house, built room upon room to achieve a fair measure of security, but not intended to withstand serious siege—was not confined to Scotland and Ireland. It was accepted also in England, where it was carried to a considerable degree of sophistication. But it was in Scotland that the idea was continued longest, the later 16th and 17th centuries seeing an exuberant revival of tower house building for reasons that were social and political rather than military.

5, 76
82

CURTAINS AND WALL TOWERS

Curtain Walls The curtain wall, though apparently often merely linking the more impressive wall towers, is the essential element of the castle. Protection comes from being enclosed, and the earliest castles consisted

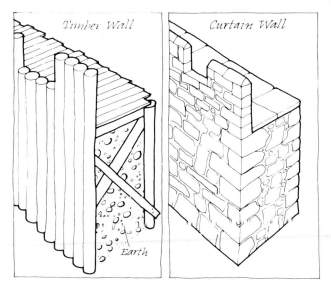

Walls of timber and stone. The eventual collapse of the timber wall will disguise its original similarity to the stone wall

merely of enclosing walls, whether built of timber or of stone.

A timber wall can be only as thick as the girth of the largest tree trunks available. For extra solidity it requires to be backed by a mass of earth (i.e., a rampart), which may itself be completely encased in timber. If the frontal timbers are carried up above the level of the earth backing they will form a breastwork, the earth backing forming a convenient sentry-walk. A stone wall, on the other hand, can resist an attack by battering ram by its own mass, is fireproof and can accommodate a sentry-walk within its thickness.

For this last purpose, the outer facing of the wall is carried up above the main body of the wall to form a parapet: the inner face may be similarly carried up to form a second parapet to the rear, called a 'parados'. To accommodate a sentry-walk a curtain wall needs to be at least 2 m (6–7 ft) thick. In practice, many curtain walls are much thicker, often measuring 4 m (13 ft) or more in width.

In order to protect the masonry against the penetration of water, the sentry-walk was sometimes covered with lead sheets. Even where these have been removed, thin grooves at the foot of the parapet or parados may 86, 99 reveal their former presence. Drain holes in the parapet should not be confused with the holes for beams to carry a hourd; usually the purpose of any holes can be decided by a moment's consideration of the way the water would tend to flow, though it must be admitted that in some cases not even experts can agree! The addition of hourds made a marked difference to the effectiveness

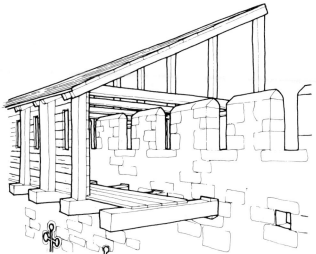

Cut-away view of a timber hourd surmounting a curtain wall

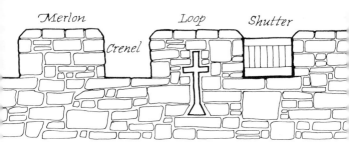

A stretch of curtain wall. Note that the crenels were often protected by wooden shutters

of the defence which could be mounted from the wall top, and their possible presence should always be borne in mind. Machicolations, the later stone replacements of hourds, are only rarely found on curtain walls, occurring usually only on keeps, wall towers and gatehouses.

When a hourd was not erected, the defence of the curtain was mounted from the sentry-walk. For this purpose the parapet was battlemented, with embrasures or 'crenels' usually just less than 1 m (c. 3 ft) wide. In the 11th and 12th centuries the solid stretches of parapet between the crenels (called 'merlons') were much wider than the crenels themselves: but by the 13th century crenels were placed closer together. For extra protection the crenel was sometimes closed by a swinging shutter hinged at the top. This could be swung open by anyone wishing to discharge a missile at those below, and while propped open protected the defender against falling arrows. To prevent arrows ricocheting off the sides of the crenel or merlon, a lip or moulding was often left protruding from it. From the beginning of the 13th century arrow-loops were also provided in the middle of each merlon, thus doubling the number of points from which archers could direct their fire from the wall top. Sometimes the tops of the merlons were treated decoratively; in some Welsh castles they bear carved heads or small pinnacles, while in some 15th-century Irish castles they have stepped tops. 88, 95 99 161, 176

The way in which the sentry-walk meets the wall towers may be treated in three different ways. Firstly, there may be no access from the sentry-walk to the tower: this enables the wall tower to hold out indefinitely should the enemy reach the sentry-walk along the curtain wall. Secondly, there may be direct access through the tower, the doors being heavily barred or even protected by small portcullises. Thirdly, the sentry-walk may be run round the back of the tower. This represents a compromise: men can then be moved swiftly from one part of the sentry-walk to another without having to descend to courtyard level, while the intervening wall towers can if necessary hold out as individual strongpoints. 11, 88 18 99, 109

Defence could also be mounted at levels below that of the wall top. Embrasures with arrow-loops could be built into the lower part of the wall, so that archers standing at ground level could add their fire to that of their comrades on the sentry-walk. However, such a practice weakens the wall at a level where an attack by battering-ram may result in a breach being made. At Caernarvon the provision of arrow-loops reaches its culmination, there being no less than three intended levels from which archers could operate: the sentry-walk itself, and two lower galleries (one unfinished) running in the thickness of the wall. 88

Wall Towers Few examples of wall towers are known from the 11th or early 12th centuries. However, recent excavations have shown that some earthwork castles were equipped with timber towers, and it may be that wall towers of stone or timber were more common at this date than the surviving evidence might lead us to believe. Those examples which do survive are 112

127

square in plan, small in size and widely spaced along the line of the curtain.

Two 12th-century examples show the curtain wall itself bent outwards and built upwards to form projecting towers open at the back towards the bailey. Here the motive was purely military: the towers have no additional value in providing accommodation. The main advance comes with King John's work at Dover at the beginning of the 13th century. Here a closely spaced series of small square open-backed towers had been built by Henry II in the 1170s. John's towers, however, are closed at the back and rounded at the front, thus producing a D-shaped tower which can be used for storage or to provide accommodation as required.

From this date the D-plan tower becomes the most
common type of wall tower, though square, polygonal and circular plans were also used. At first the lower part

Spurred wall towers of the later 13th century at Goodrich, Herefordshire

of the tower was solid, only the upper part being built hollow: subsequently towers were built with accommodation on three or four storeys. The lower part of the front of the tower, always the most vulnerable, is sometimes protected by pyramidal spurs of masonry which project towards the field so as to deflect stones hurled by *petraria*. Since the fronts of wall towers are sometimes carried down into the ditch or moat, the lowest storey may be either at the level of the bailey or sunk lower as a basement. 33, 95 113

Inter-level communication is by stairs. These may be spiral stairs of the usual kind, rising from beside the door into the lowest storey, or they may rise in short flights within the thickness of the wall. Spiral stairs may finish in small turrets rising above the roof level of the main tower. The shape of the roof can only rarely be even surmised: whereas conical roofs may give a more pleasing aspect to the castle, flat roofs are more practical in time of war since they allow the rapid movement of men from one side to another and since small *petraria* can be mounted there. 11, 140 187 11, 88 99

The rooms inside wall towers may be used for a great variety of purposes—storage, imprisonment, casual accommodation, chapels, kitchens or the permanent accommodation of the lord of the castle himself. A castle such as Bodiam shows all these uses applied to its various towers. A careful study of the way in which the rooms in a tower open off the stair, the degrees of privacy thus achieved, the presence or absence of such amenities as fireplaces and latrines, will usually reveal the purpose to which a tower was put. Occasionally it is possible to find a single tower functioning as a complete house set on end, with storage basement, kitchen, hall and chamber rather in the fashion of a small keep. Indeed, some large wall towers should perhaps be counted as keeps set on the line of the curtain. 11 95 80, 88 141

The primary function of a wall tower, however, is

129

to allow archers to command the face of the adjoining curtain. The most convenient place from which to do so was the roof of the tower, and many wall towers are surprisingly 'blind' at lower levels. Usually, however, there is at least one arrow-loop near the angle between tower and curtain wall on each storey, from which an archer could fire along the face of the curtain. A pattern of three loops on each floor is common, two being at the sides of the tower and one in front towards the field (facing directly outwards). Massed loops are rare, though some of Edward I's Welsh castles made provision for a considerable number of archers.

Wall towers, like the curtain wall itself, form part of the basic structure of the castle. Once the idea had been evolved or rediscovered, wall towers became a necessary part of every castle built during the Middle Ages.

GATEHOUSES

Gatehouses Even the simplest of castles boasted a gatehouse. Indeed, it is possible that from the very beginning the gatehouse epitomized the rest of the castle's defence and so came to represent power and lordship in the period before the evolution of the keep. A few timber gate towers are known from excavation. The earliest surviving stone examples are square or nearly square in plan, some with pilaster buttresses. They vary in size from 8 to 15 m (c. 26 to 50 ft) square, rising through two or three storeys to as much as 25 m (more than 80 ft) in height. The ground floor contains the gate passage, which is sometimes (but not always) vaulted as a protection against fire. The entrance passages are defended by drawbridges and wooden doors and, in at least one instance, by a portcullis. In the larger gatehouses the upper storeys may have provided some of the best accommodation in the castle. With these, a common fate is for the entrance passage to have been blocked in the late 12th century, with a new gate in-

Reconstruction of an early stone gatehouse, based on Exeter, Devon

serted in the curtain wall alongside and the gate tower
46, 66 itself heightened to form a small keep.

By the end of the 12th century experiments were
being made with gates with small towers or turrets
27, 42 placed each side of them. The towers may be solid or
45 open, square or round in plan. Early in the 13th century
such towers were joined above the entrance passage to
8, 82 form a gatehouse with two projecting towers flanking
the approach. The towers are usually rounded towards
the field, though they may also be polygonal, and flat-
backed towards the bailey. Such gatehouses often contain accommodation of some comfort in the room
above the gate passage and in the upper parts of the
towers: traditionally, this was the lodging of the con-

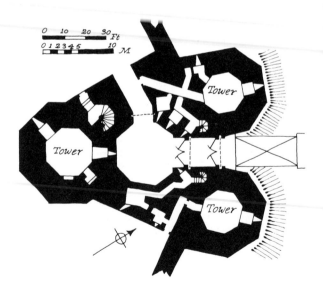

Denbigh, Clwyd: plan of the three-towered gatehouse

stable of the castle, unless he had a suite of rooms else-where.

The approach to the gatehouse is often covered by a barbican and by a drawbridge (see below). Within the vaulted gate passage there may be traces of several sets of doors and several portcullises, their position being shown by the rebates against which the doors closed and by the sockets for the locking bars, or by the grooves in which the portcullis worked. Openings in the vault (often called *meurtrières* or 'murder holes') were prob-ably for pouring water to extinguish fires rather than for the boiling oil of popular imagination.

The sequence of doors and portcullises may be very complex. In Edward I's Welsh castles there are often as many as three pairs of doors and three portcul-lises. The triangular gatehouse at Denbigh is built to a particularly fearsome plan. The drawbridge rose against the outer face of the gatehouse, in effect forming an extra door. Within there are two further sets of doors and two portcullises controlling access to a large octa-gonal vaulted room in the centre of the building. This is commanded by five arrow-loops, and must have been a lethal place for an attacker. Entry to the bailey is through another passage leading out of the central space at right angles to the first: now largely destroyed, it probably incorporated more doors and portcullises. It is probable that the unfinished King's Gate at Caernar-von was intended to follow this pattern.

The gatehouses of some of Edward I's Welsh castles are so large as to have been able to offer a great deal of accommodation, and for this reason are sometimes called 'gatehouse keeps'. They represent a reversion to the 11th-century idea whereby the strongest building in the castle protected the gate, rather than standing within the inner bailey. At Beaumaris, left unfinished, there were intended to be at least five separate suites of rooms in the two identical gatehouses. Here once again,

88, 109

102

88

86, 109

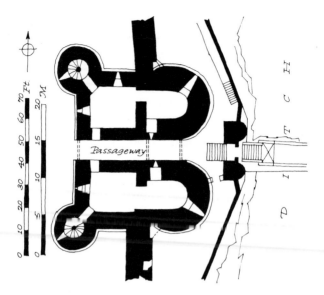

Harlech, Gwynedd: plan of the great gatehouse

it is necessary to look carefully at the stair links, the way in which doors opened into, or out of, a room, and the provision of fireplaces, window-seats and latrines, in order to discern the type of accommodation they offered.

Not all gatehouses are so grand as these, though some copy the plan on a smaller scale. In almost all of them, the rooms above the gate passage are built as halls, with linking chambers in the towers and spiral stairs placed in turrets rising against the rear wall.

The arrow-loops commanding at ground level the approach to the drawbridge are sometimes converted to allow for the use of hand-guns. Sometimes, too, the gatehouse has been reduced in height in an attempt to render it proof against cannon fire. All too rarely is a medieval gatehouse now seen complete to its full height, with battlements and machicolations intact.

Drawbridges Drawbridges were of four main types. The simplest was just a retractable gangplank forming the inner section of a wooden bridge across the moat or ditch: the outer part of the bridge remained in position all the time. Such bridges needed no special architectural arrangements and few positive traces of them now remain.

'Lifting bridges' were hinged at their inner end on the threshold of the gatehouse, being raised by chains worked from a windlass operating in the first floor room above the gate passage. Most early castles were probably fitted with this sort of drawbridge, which works well when kept small in size: for this reason the type was retained in later castles for the bridges of postern gates, which were smaller than those of the main gatehouses.

Where the gatehouse was large, the gate passage correspondingly high, and the moat or ditch wide, a longer drawbridge was needed. This might be heavier than could be raised with a simple windlass, and so a 'turning bridge' was used. The bridge was extended backwards into the gate passage and a counterweight was placed on its inner end. The bridge still pivoted at the threshold of the gatehouse, but it swung like a seesaw: as the outer part of the bridge rose up, so the inner part dropped down into a pit dug in the gate passage just inside the threshold. Such pits, in addition to being necessary to receive the counterbalanced inner end of the bridge, also formed an obstacle to an attacker. Usually, the inner part of the bridge was made slightly heavier than the outer part, it being necessary to lock it in position when lowered by passing a wooden bar under its end. Removal of the bar allowed the counterbalance to drop

88, 102
132, 190

135

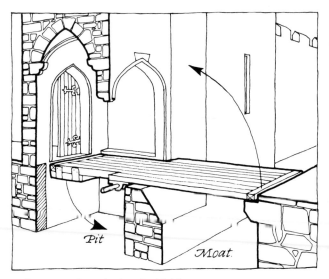

Cut-away view of a 'turning' bridge

down into the pit, so causing the outer part of the bridge to rise. Once risen, the outer part was locked in position by a second wooden bar slid across its outer face from one of the flanking towers of the gatehouse.

Some builders, however, seem to have considered the pit for the counterbalance more trouble than it was worth. A compromise was devised whereby separate 33, 52 counterbalances were mounted on three long beams 80 projecting backwards from the bridge into the gate passage. For these no pit was necessary, merely three slots into which the weighted beams might drop.

Even these, however, might incommode the defenders, and during the early 14th century a new type of lifting mechanism was devised. This still depended

Cut-away view of a 'bascule' bridge

upon long beams with counterbalance weights, but now the beams were pivoted just above the top of the gate opening. When the bridge was down, the outer ends of the beams projected horizontally from the gate-house some 3 m (*c.* 10 ft) above the bridge, and were connected to its outer end by chains. When the inner ends of the beams were allowed to drop down from their position just below the vault or ceiling of the gate passage, the outer ends rose up, lifting the bridge with them. Such counterbalanced lifting bridges can still be seen in use over Dutch canals. Their former existence in British castles can be detected by the two vertical slots cut in the stonework of the outer face of the gatehouse just above the entrance arch: these slots received the outer ends of the beams when the bridge was raised, allowing the bridge itself to rest flush against the stonework. Bridges of this type are called bascule bridges.

No drawbridges of medieval date survive. Often, later modifications of the gatehouse have led to the filling in of the counterbalance pit or of the recesses for the lifting beams. In most cases, however, careful examination of the stonework will reveal at least which type of drawbridge was used, even if the details cannot be ascertained.

Portcullises and Yetts A portcullis is a gate which can be lowered into position from above. It is not hinged, but slides in a groove cut in the stonework at each side of the passage it is intended to block. No portcullis of medieval date is known for certain to survive: the few still in position are probably 16th-century or later replacements. The portcullis is a frame or grid of stout timbers held together by iron nails or clamps. The lower ends of the upright timbers were sharpened to a point and shod with iron, so that when the portcullis was allowed to drop—which was usually in an emergency—it would skewer anyone standing beneath. The great advantage of the portcullis over the gate was thus that it could be dropped into position very quickly, and that its dropping could not be resisted. Once in position it could not be burst open by an attacker, as could a hinged door or gate, but had to be dismantled or burned.

The portcullis was raised by a windlass working directly above it in the room over the gate passage, or in a room above that. When raised sufficiently to allow mounted men and loaded carts to pass underneath, the upper part at least projected through a slot in the vault or ceiling of the gate passage into the room above. Very few examples of such windlasses survive. Where they 80 do survive, they inevitably take up a good deal of space.

Often the room above the gate passage was a chapel, and the portcullis with its winding gear must have contrasted oddly with the altar and its fittings. Here was militant Christianity indeed.

Portcullises were known to the Romans, but appear commonly in Britain only from the middle of the 45 12th century. From the beginning of the 13th century onwards, few gatehouses were without at least one portcullis, and many had three or more (see 'Gatehouses', page 130). In the north of England and in Scotland the place of the portcullis is often taken by the **Yett,** a gate in the form of an iron grille, hinged like a door, 133 of which a number still survive. This may be secured by iron bolts, or by a timber bar sliding in a socket cut into the stone jamb. In Scotland the iron bars of the grille are passed through each other: in England the vertical bars pass in front of the horizontals and the grille is often backed by boards to form an iron-laced door.

Barbicans   The function of the barbican is twofold. Firstly it provides an outer defence for the main gate, thus preventing a sudden attack carrying the gatehouse before the defenders can respond. Secondly, it confines those who are attacking the main gate to a small area just in front of the gate where the maximum defensive fire-power may be deployed.

There are two basic types of barbican. One consists of an outer enclosure, defended by its own rampart or curtain wall and with its own gatehouse, set on the outer 38, 89 side of the main ditch, astride the approach to the drawbridge of the main gatehouse. This outer enclosure may be large, almost forming an extra bailey, or small, 11, 33 merely protecting the outer end of the drawbridge. A variant of the latter form is an enclosure lying on the same side of the ditch as the main gatehouse, i.e., not 27, 66 divided from it by a ditch, but merely providing an 99 extra 'layer' of defence beyond the gate.

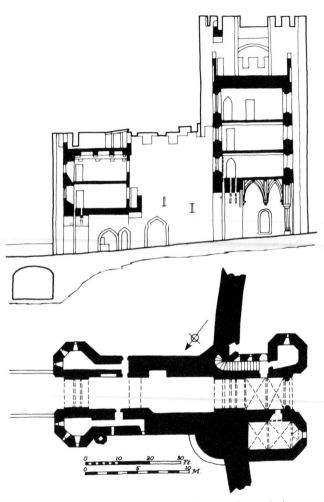

The gatehouse and barbican at Warwick: section and plan

The second type consists of a narrow open passage 23, 43
bounded by walls and projecting forward from the 190
main gatehouse, being closed at its outer end by a
second gate or even a second gatehouse. Such barbicans
would force an enemy intent on attacking the main gate
into a selected 'killing ground'. The most remarkable
example of this feature is at Warwick. Here the open 83
passage in front of the main gatehouse is flanked by tall
side walls having crenels to both parapet and parados,
so that archers could fire into the passage as well as out
towards the field. The outer end of this killing ground
is blocked by a three-storey gatehouse. An enemy who
succeeded in crossing the ditch and passing the portcullis
and doors blocking the entrance passage through this
gatehouse found himself in a killing ground some 8 m
($c.$ 26 ft) long and 3 m ($c.$ 10 ft) wide, where he would
be under fire from the great inner gatehouse in front
of him, from the tops of the walls on either side, and
from the top of the barbican gatehouse, behind him.

Variations on this type of barbican abound. The barbican gatehouse may be rectangular in plan, or round. 95, 190
It may have small projecting turrets, or be quite plain. 43, 83
There may be no barbican gatehouse as such at all, the
killing ground being closed at its outer end merely by
a strong gate flanked by small round turrets. The killing
ground may be reduced in length to only a few metres,
or it may be drawn out to a great length. Only the
Tower of London combines both the basic types. 80

HALLS, KITCHENS AND CHAPELS

Halls Well preserved castle halls are a rarity: too
often the hall has been either reduced to a set of low
footings or else so altered by later occupants as to be
almost unrecognizable. Frequently the position formerly occupied by the hall is indicated only by a few
large windows, and perhaps a fireplace or two, still

surviving in the stonework of the curtain wall against which the hall was built.

The two basic types of hall—that in which the lord's hall and chamber are raised to first-floor level, and that in which the hall is at ground level, the lord's chamber lying at first-floor level above the service rooms at one end of the hall—have been discussed in Chapter V.

The 'houses in the castle' differed from contemporary undefended houses only in the way in which they were made to fit within a preconceived plan dictated by the defences. Except where security demanded it the windows, doors and other architectural items are identical with those found elsewhere. For this reason no detailed description is attempted here: instead the reader is

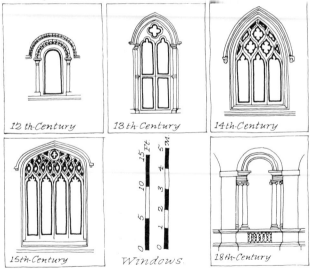

Types of window to be seen in the domestic buildings of castles

referred to the companion *Observer's Book of Architecture*. As a guide to the basic types, however, it should be noted that Norman windows and doors were topped by semicircular arches. Early examples, or examples where good stone for carving was not available, may be relatively plain: later, in the 12th century, considerable enrichment was provided in the form of carving around the arch itself and small columns attached to the sides of the opening. Towards the end of the 12th century the 'Gothic' style became popular. Windows and doors were contained within elaborately decorated pointed arches. The form of the decoration—the shape of the mouldings round the jambs, the pattern of the stone tracery—gives the expert an indication of the date at which the stones were carved. Later medieval doors and windows show a flatter pointed arch, sometimes (though erroneously) known as a 'Tudor arch'. Many castles were modified after the end of the Middle Ages. Care should be taken not to confuse the neo-Roman round-headed arches of the 17th and 18th centuries with those of Norman date: these later insertions will be of sharply square-cut stone, often with exaggerated key-stones.

Kitchens   Kitchens were built wherever they were needed to provide hot food. They thus adjoin the main domestic accommodation and the more formal hall, but may be built separately in the bailey, attached to the range of buildings containing the hall itself, or tucked into a wall tower. They may be small or large, depending upon the number of people to be fed from the particular kitchen in question. Where there are separate 'houses in the castle', there will usually be more than 11 one kitchen. Similar duplication can be found in some 58 keeps. In tower houses kitchens were contrived in small spaces screened off at one end of the hall, or occupy a 126, 130 room in a 'jamb'.

Kitchens are recognizable primarily by the size of their fireplaces, which are much larger than the fireplaces found in halls and chambers, being designed for the roasting of complete oxen. (King John even ordered the construction of ovens large enough to take two or three oxen at once!) A width of 2–3 m (c. 6–10 ft) is thus not uncommon. The back of the fireplace will frequently be lined with tiles set so as to present only their edges to the heat. Small bread ovens, similarly lined with tiles, may open off the back of the fireplace. A large kitchen may have two or even three such fireplaces, generally set at opposite sides of the room.

11, 58
113

Only rarely do ancillary details survive, such as sinks and drains, or serving hatches. An essential item was a well: this may be in the kitchen itself, but more often is to be found nearby, allowing access both from the kitchen and from other parts of the castle.

58, 133

27, 68
33, 66
11, 121
46, 84

Chapels Chapels may be found in the forebuildings and upper chambers of keeps, in wall towers and gatehouses, attached to the lord's hall and chamber, or standing free in the bailey. This results in many variations in plan. Where the chapel stands as a separate building in the bailey it may echo the plan of chapels and churches built at the same time in towns and villages. In all other cases the plan is dictated by considerations other than those of rite or liturgy: only the orientation towards the east remains a common feature, and sometimes the shape of the space into which a chapel has had to be crammed precludes even this.

Rarely will an altar survive, though there may be a modern replacement. The main indications that the room was used as a chapel will be the presence of a *piscina* (a stone basin for rinsing out the chalice after Mass) or a *sedilia* (a row of stone seats along one side of the room for the use of the priest, deacon and subdeacon). There may also be decorative arcading—some-

144

Piscina and sedilia

times called 'blind' arcading—along the walls, with semicircular (Norman) or pointed (Gothic) arches according to the architectural fashion then prevailing. The roof will usually be vaulted, the choice of a rounded 'barrel' vault or pointed Gothic vault again depending upon date and fashion. Both Norman and Gothic vaults may be intersected by small cross-vaults, with the edges of their intersections enriched with moulded ribs.

In the larger castles there will often be a small vestry or sacristy for the keeping of vestments, books and sacred vessels, opening off the chapel. More rarely a lodging for the chaplain can be found. Where the chapel is in a gatehouse, or in the forebuilding of a keep, there may be provision for working a portcullis. Usually, only the slot in the floor against one wall will survive to show that this was the case.

11, 23
113

58, 67
113

145

LOOPS

Arrow-Loops Arrow-loops enable a defender to fire at an attacker without exposing himself to the degree that would be necessary were he to lean over the battlements. The opening in the outer face of the walls is kept narrow, perhaps only 5–10 cm (*c*. 2–4 in.) wide. Care must be taken not to confuse arrow-loops with what may be described as 'high security windows'. These latter often resemble arrow-loops from the outside: inside, the jambs are splayed to admit as much air and light as possible, but even so an archer could not stand close enough to the opening to direct his fire with any accuracy. Most 11th- and early 12th-century 'loops' are in fact windows. The true arrow-loop is marked by the wider space or *embrasure* hollowed in the thickness of

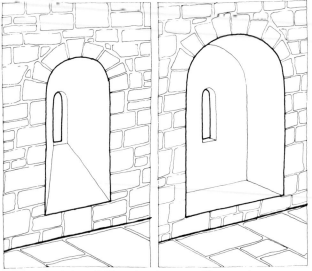

Splayed window (left) and embrasure with arrow-loop (right)

the wall behind so that an archer—particularly one armed with crossbow—could operate with greater ease.

Such loops, backed by embrasures, occur only sporadically in the 11th and early 12th centuries. By the beginning of the 13th century they were more common, being sometimes equipped with cross-slits: one medieval writer says that this was specifically for the more effective use of crossbows. The bottom of the vertical slit was also splayed slightly to allow the archer to depress his angle of fire sufficiently to be able to hit anyone standing near the foot of the wall. Later in the 13th century the ends of the slits forming the loop were cut in the form of a small circular opening.

Behind the loop itself the embrasure was usually quite plain, having a flat lintel or a low arch. An early

22, 38
81, 116
148

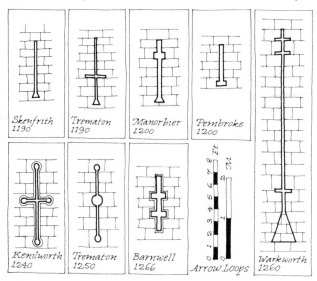

Types of arrow-loop, 12th and 13th centuries

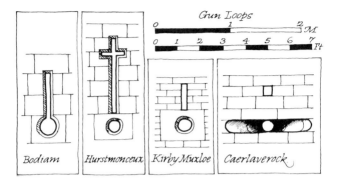

Types of gun-loop, 14th and 15th centuries

27 experiment was the opening of three loops from a single embrasure, thus enormously increasing the archer's field of fire. The reverse is also found—three
88 embrasures (i.e., firing positions) utilizing a single loop— the object again being to allow the archer to command a greater field.

Gun-Loops In England the first loops specifically
11 for the discharge of hand-guns occur at the end of the
146, 176 14th century. By the 1460s they were in use in Scotland and Ireland. The earliest form resembles an inverted keyhole when viewed from the outside. Later, the observation slit is made separate from the circular opening for the barrel of the gun itself. By the end of the 15th century the whole idea of the old arrow-loop was being reversed: the gun worked in a horizontal or oval loop splayed not on the inside, but on the outside. Within the embrasure behind the loop there can often be seen a slot in the masonry where a horizontal wooden sill was placed to receive the spike in the gun's swivel support.

148

VII ON YOUR OWN

By the time you reach this point you should be ready to go out and analyse a castle on your own. The Gazetteer on pages 156–183 will give you an idea of the variety of castles awaiting you. The Site Lists on pages 184–185 will help you if you want to start by looking at a particular type of castle, and the Maps on the endpapers will show which castles lie nearest your home. However, these are only a small part of the great wealth of castles that exists in Great Britain and Ireland. The exact number has never been calculated, but there are probably over 1000 earthwork castles and 500 or 600 stone castles still surviving. This book can therefore provide only a starting point for your researches.

Before setting out, it is worthwhile consulting a history of the county in which the castle you intend to visit lies. Alternatively, you may be able to obtain a guide-book in advance by writing to the organizations mentioned in Chapter I. From these sources, you will, if you are lucky, get some idea of the people who lived in the castle, and perhaps even the name of the man who built it. You will have to be careful here. Many castles were in existence for a century or more before being mentioned in a medieval document and so coming to the attention of the historian. Even when there survives a specific 'licence to crenellate' (i.e., a royal permit to fortify a house or build a new castle) bearing a precise date, the nature of such licences must be borne in mind. The castle may have been built during the reign of an earlier weaker king, the owner later deeming it prudent to get retrospective royal approval from a stronger successor. On the other hand, an ambitious lord may have taken the trouble to get royal assent for the building of a castle, only to find it was many years before he could find the resources to erect it. Some licences were never used at all.

So do not be afraid to trust the evidence of the buildings themselves rather than the evidence of the written sources. Make a checklist of things to look for and work through it systematically.

When you reach the castle, look first at its position. Is it in a town of medieval origin, or is it in open country? Is it set on top of an inaccessible hill, or does it stand in lush pastures? Look to see how it makes use of the shape of the land. Does it use cliffs and steep slopes to keep the enemy away from its walls, or is it built in a valley where water could be brought to fill a moat?

These facts will help to tell you why the first castle was built on that particular site: whether its purpose was to guard a town or a narrow pass: to prevent raiders passing up a river which was once navigable but which may now be merely a stream: or whether it was designed primarily to act as the defensive and administrative centre of a great estate.

To note these details, always walk right round the castle on the outside before going in. Use the opportunity to see how effective the defences are. Would it be easy to divert the stream feeding the moat and so dry it out? Is there a barbican? How tall is the curtain wall? Are the wall towers closely spaced, or are there blind spots? Can you see any provision for the erection of timber hourds? Is there any high ground within 100 m (*c.* 110 yd) from which stone-throwing *petraria* could pound the walls? Make a sketch plan, noting the shape of the towers and any changes of alignment in the curtain wall.

By the time you have finished your circuit round the

castle you should have got some idea of the strength of the castle in its heyday, and also of its general form. If you can see a motte, then its bailey will probably have dictated the plan of any later defences. A large, sprawling castle, with great lengths of curtain wall sparsely studded with towers of varying shape, suggests a long

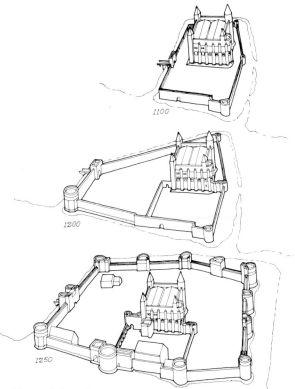

The evolution of a royal fortress: three stages in the development of the Tower of London

151

and possibly involved building history, with extra baileys added and lodgings spaced about the various courtyards. A compact quadrilateral, surrounded by a moat, will indicate a later medieval work, with all the buildings dovetailed into a convenient and coherent plan.

Inside the castle, look at the general disposition of the buildings. Is there a keep? Add it to your sketch plan. The plan of a castle is always the best clue to its overall history and development. Armed with some sort of plan you can start working out how this particular castle was used.

Look for the great hall. If there is a keep there will be one there, but there may also be another hall in the bailey. If it is at ground level look for a screens passage and service rooms: look for a great kitchen for those formal banquets. Note that even when the domestic buildings have been demolished there will often be stairs, windows, fireplaces and latrines surviving in the curtain wall against which they once stood. Look for the horizontal rows of square holes to receive the floor joists of upper rooms. Many guide-books will show only a plan taken at ground level. If you do not look up as well as down you will miss half the accommodation the castle once offered.

Look at the wall towers from both the military and the domestic point of view. How good a field of fire is there from each loop and crenel? How easy is it to get onto the sentry-walk along the top of the curtain? Do the rooms in the towers have fireplaces and latrines? Is there a separate stair, or do you have to go through each room on your way to the battlements?

Find the chapel in the bailey. Look for private chapels in the keep or gatehouse. How many wells are there? How vulnerable was the defenders' water supply?

Look for later alterations to the buildings. Enlarged

windows may indicate not only a change in fashion and a desire for greater comfort; if they occur below second-floor level in the outer walls they indicate a change in the owner's attitude towards his castle and the role it was expected to play in military affairs. Look for buildings that have been heightened. This can be deduced from changes in the masonry or in the style of the windows in the upper part of the building. Look for traces of buildings that have been torn down. These will have left scars in the masonry of surviving walls, where the stones of the missing wall were bonded-in. There may also be old roof lines where the lead 'flashing' was grooved into the stonework.

Look, too, for signs of any reuse of the castle during the Civil War of the 17th century. Look for towers cut down to a more squat profile as a defence against gunfire. Look for army barracks built in the bailey or in the keep. Look for the sharp-angled earthworks thrown up round the castle to protect gun batteries.

Lastly, try to find out why the castle fell into disuse. Has it been deliberately 'slighted' so that it could not be used again? Do the latest traces of use suggest that the buildings were too expensive to keep up? Are there people still living in it, so that it is only the military aspects which have fallen into disuse?

As you leave, look back and try to visualize the growth and development of the castle on that site: its impact, and the impact of its occupants, on the neighbouring towns and villages: the ways in which the occupants drew on the countryside around for fuel, food and sport. Try to imagine, too, the converse of all this: the slow decline into disuse, the collapse of some buildings and the deliberate destruction of others for the materials they contained. Think of the society which came to rely on such massive devices of war, and then came to realise they were no longer necessary.

153

GLOSSARY

Aisled divided into three parts longitudinally by two arcades supporting the roof

Apse the rounded east wall of a church or chapel

Arcade a row of arches, 'blind' when applied to a wall for decorative purposes

Bailey the defended courtyard of a castle

Barbican a small outer fortification protecting a gate or drawbridge

Batter an inward slope to a wall face

Chamber a private room.

Constable the official in charge of a castle in the absence of its owner

Corbel a projecting stone to carry a beam: several tiers of corbels may carry a parapet or a turret

Crenel a square notch in a parapet. A row of crenels produce 'battlements'

Donjon a medieval word for a keep, with connotations of lordship

Embrasure (i) crenel (ii) space hollowed in a thick wall to allow an archer to stand closer to a loop

Forebuilding a building projecting from the face of a keep, containing the entrance stair

Garderobe latrine (literally a 'wardrobe')

Hall a formal reception room for the holding of courts and the entertainment of guests

Hourd an overhanging timber gallery projecting from the top of a wall

Jamb the side of a door or window opening. Also (in Scotland) the projecting wing of a tower house

Keep the main tower of a castle, often isolated and capable of independent defence. A shell keep (really a misnomer) results from the replacement in stone of a timber palisade on a motte

Lintel the flat top of a door or window opening

Loop a narrow opening in a wall for the discharge of missiles

Machicolation   an overhanging parapet pierced for dropping stones and other missiles

Merlon   the short length of a parapet between crenels

Motte   a large earth mound for the support of a timber tower

Oratory   a small private chamber for prayer

Parados   a stone breastwork protecting the rear of a sentry-walk

Parapet   a stone breastwork protecting the front of a sentry-walk

Pilaster   a flat decorative buttress, often found on keeps

Piscina   a stone basin in a chapel, for rinsing sacred vessels

Portcullis   a wooden grille sliding vertically in grooves cut in the stonework of a gate passage

Putlog holes   holes left by the withdrawal of timbers used to secure scaffolding

Sedilia   a row of stone seats against the south wall of a chapel

Slighting   the deliberate demolition of a castle to prevent further use

Vault   an arched roof usually of stone. A 'barrel' vault has a semicircular arch, and a 'Gothic' vault a pointed arch

Window seat   a stone seat built into the jamb of a window

Yett   an iron gate found in tower houses

GAZETTEER

Note: Castles in State care in England are marked EH (English Heritage); in Scotland, SDD (Scottish Development Department); in Wales, C (Cadw); in Northern Ireland, DOE (Department of the Environment); and in the Republic of Ireland, OPW (Office of Public Works). Castles maintained by the National Trust are marked NT. All other castles are maintained by local authorities or private owners. The letters and figures in brackets, immediately following a castle's location, are the National Grid reference.

ENGLAND

1 Castle Acre, *Norfolk, 6·4 km (4 miles) N of Swaffham (TF 820132)* Ringwork with square bailey. Large square hall house of later 11th century within ringwork, converted to keep early in 12th century. Remains of octagonal curtain wall round ringwork, and of polygonal curtain wall round bailey. Foundations of hall visible in bailey. (EH)

2 Acton Burnell, *Salop, 12·8 km (8 miles) S of Shrewsbury (SJ 534019)* Elaborate fortified house of 1280s. Main block is of two storeys in eastern part and three storeys in western part: square projecting corner towers of four storeys. (EH)

3 Appleby, *Cumbria, 22·5 km (14 miles) SE of Penrith (NY 685199)* Ringwork with rectangular bailey, with plain curtain of 12th century. Square keep of three storeys, heightened in 13th century and altered in 17th century. D-plan wall tower of 13th century and two square corner towers of 15th century. Hall of 15th century incorporated in large house of 17th century in bailey.

4 Arundel, *W Sussex (TQ 018073)* Tall motte with two baileys. Shell keep of late 11th or early 12th century on motte, with square wall tower commanding entrance. Curtain wall of same date, with one square wall tower, survives round northern bailey; square gatehouse to southern bailey of *c.* 1100. Castle much altered in 19th century, when rebuilt in Neo-Gothic style.

5 Ashby de la Zouche, *Leicestershire, 19·3 km (12 miles) NW of Leicester (SK 363167)* Rectangular moated manor (defences now obliterated) with two courtyards. Hall, buttery and pantry of 12th century, rebuilt in late 14th century when kitchen and solar added. Chapel and tower house of late 15th century. (EH)

6 Bamburgh, *Northumberland (NU 184350)* Irregular elongated enclosure divided into three parts, on rock occupied since at least 6th century. Square keep of three storeys (later heightened) possibly of early 12th century. Curtain with square and D-plan wall towers: barbican and outer gatehouse of 13th century. Domestic buildings and chapel of 13th century. Castle extensively 'restored' in 19th century.

7 Barnard Castle, *Durham, 24 km (15 miles) SW of Bishop Auckland (NZ 049165)* Ringwork with large sub-rectangular bailey, divided into three separate parts: remains of curtain of early 12th century. Ringwork has curtain of early or mid 12th century and later domestic range: large round wall tower of three storeys (built *c.* 1240) serves as keep and chamber block at end of early 14th-century hall. (EH)

8 Beeston, *Cheshire, 24 km (15 miles) SE of Chester (SJ 537593)* Large outer bailey with curtain and D-plan wall towers. Inner bailey utilizes cliffs on two sides: curtain and gatehouse of early 13th century, with one square and one D-plan wall tower. (EH)

9 Berkeley, *Gloucestershire, 35·4 km (22 miles) NE of Bristol (ST 684990)* Motte and bailey. Motte revetted in stone to form shell keep with three half-round projecting turrets and forebuilding containing stair. Remains of 11th-century hall in bailey.

10 Berkhamsted, *Hertfordshire, 6·4 km (4 miles) W of Hemel Hempstead (SP 995082)* Tall motte with oval bailey, surrounded by moat with outer rampart and ditch. Foundations of shell keep on motte. Curtain wall with D-plan wall towers and one square keep-like tower. Outer earthwork with projecting platforms, possibly siege work of 1216. (EH)

11 Bodiam, *E Sussex, 19·3 km (12 miles) N of Hastings (TQ 785256)* Quadrangular castle of late 14th century, surrounded by moat. Four ranges of two-storey buildings (now ruined) set round courtyard, with round corner towers and

157

intermediary square wall towers. Machicolated gatehouse and postern tower, and small barbican gatehouse. (NT)

12 Bolingbroke, *Lincolnshire, 4·8 km (3 miles) SW of Spilsby (TF 348654)* Irregular hexagonal bailey, formerly surrounded by moat, with D-plan corner towers and gatehouse of early 13th century. One tower rebuilt in octagonal form in 1450. Foundations of hall of 15th century. Much ruined. (EH)

13 Bolton-in-Wensleydale, *N Yorkshire, 27·3 km (17 miles) SW of Richmond (SE 034918)* Quadrangular castle of later 14th century. Four ranges of three-storey buildings set round courtyard, with rectangular corner towers of five storeys. Elaborate domestic planning, with numerous halls and chambers.

14 Caister by Yarmouth, *Norfolk, 8 km (5 miles) NW of Yarmouth (TA 116012)* Moated quadrangular castle of early 15th century. Only the west front survives, with machicolated curtain and gatehouse. A narrow round corner tower of five storeys served as a chamber block adjoining the hall.

15 Canterbury, *Kent (TR 146575)* Only the keep survives, built early in 12th century. Square plan, originally three storeys (top storey destroyed in 19th century).

16 Carisbrooke, *Isle of Wight (SZ 488878)* Motte with two baileys on site of Roman fort. Polygonal shell keep on motte: curtain and open-backed square corner towers of early 12th century round western bailey. Gatehouse of 13th century. Domestic buildings and chapel of 12th–14th centuries, much rebuilt in 16th century. Outer earthwork defences of 17th century. (EH)

17 Carlisle, *Cumbria (NY 396564)* Triangular enclosure with irregular outer bailey. Square keep of four storeys, and curtain with rectangular turrets of 12th century. Gatehouse of 13th century with inward barbican, and two gatehouses of 14th century. Much rebuilding in 16th century for artillery defence. (EH)

18 Chilham, *Kent, 11·2 km (7 miles) SW of Canterbury (TR 066535)* Rectangular bailey with late medieval curtain wall. Late 11th-century hall partly demolished and buried in motte. Octagonal keep with pilaster buttresses built on motte in 1170s, with projecting stair turret and latrine.

19 Chipchase, *Northumberland, 12·8 km (8 miles) NW of Hexham (NY 883757)*   Late 13th-century rectangular tower house of four storeys, with corbelled-out round corner turrets and massive machicolation between. Jacobean house of 1621 added at east end of an early 16th-century wing projecting from tower house.

20 Christchurch, *Hampshire (SZ 160926)*   Motte and bailey. Remains of rectangular keep, lower part buried in motte. First-floor hall of *c.* 1160s stands in bailey. (EH)

21 Clun, *Salop, 24 km (15 miles) NE of Ludlow (SO 298809)*   Large low motte with two baileys. Remains of curtain wall on motte, with entrance protected by half-round towers. Rectangular keep of four storeys built on side of motte.

22 Colchester, *Essex (TL 998252)*   Huge hall-keep of 1080s (now a museum). Possibly intended to be lower, but heightened in late 11th or early 12th century. Bailey almost obliterated: rampart survives on two sides. Top storey of keep demolished in 18th century.

23 Conisbrough, *S Yorkshire, 8 km (5 miles) SW of Doncaster (SK 517989)*   Oval bailey with curtain wall, small solid half-round wall towers and narrow barbican. Round keep of four storeys with six massive projecting buttresses, built *c.* 1180–90. (EH)

24 Corfe, *Dorset, 8 km (5 miles) SE of Wareham (SY 958823)*   Oval ringwork of 11th century, with curtain of same date, square keep of early 12th century, and lavish domestic buildings of early 13th century. Middle and outer baileys of 13th century, with gatehouses and D-plan wall towers. Much damaged in Civil War and subsequently slighted. (EH)

25 Deal, *Kent (TR 378521)*   Artillery fort built *c.* 1540. Circular central 'keep' with six attached gun bastions, within outer ring of six lower crescent-shaped bastions surrounded by dry ditch. (EH)

26 Donnington, *Berkshire, 3·2 km (2 miles) NW of Newbury (SU 461692)*   D-plan bailey, with curtain wall and square and round wall towers of early 14th century. Tall gatehouse of three storeys, with attached four-storey turrets, of *c.* 1386. Domestic buildings destroyed. Outer earthwork defences of 17th century. (EH)

27 Dover, *Kent (TR 326417)*   Large irregular outer bailey on lines of prehistoric hill fort, enclosing Roman lighthouse and late Saxon church. Elaborate square keep of three storeys, curtain with square open-backed wall towers and barbicans, all of late 12th century. Outer curtain with D-plan wall towers of early 13th century. Many later additions, especially in 19th century. (EH)

28 Dunstanburgh, *Northumberland, 11·2 km (7 miles) NE of Alnwick (NU 258220)*   Huge irregular bailey on edge of cliff. Curtain and square wall towers of early 13th century. Great gatehouse of early 14th century, blocked and converted to keep in 1380s, when new gate with barbican built nearby. Small inner bailey, with curtain and square corner tower, of late 14th century. (EH)

29 Durham, *Co. Durham (NZ 274423)*   Tall motte with triangular bailey. Octagonal shell keep with pilaster buttresses on motte. Curtain of later 11th or early 12th century. 11th-century chapel. Hall of later 12th century, and great hall, kitchen and domestic buildings of later 13th century. Many later alterations and additions.

30 Exeter, *Devon (SX 921929)*   Sub-rectangular ringwork in corner of Roman and late Saxon city defences. Curtain, square gatehouse and wall tower of late 11th or early 12th century. Outer bailey obliterated except for one fragment of curtain wall.

31 Farnham, *Surrey (SU 837473)*   Motte with triangular bailey, within large irregular outer enclosure with curtain wall and square wall towers. Motte revetted in stone in 13th century to form shell keep with projecting square turrets: foundations of earlier 12th century square keep (demolished *c.* 1155) built at same time as motte. Domestic buildings in bailey much altered in 17th century. (EH, part only)

32 Framlingham, *Suffolk, 24 km (15 miles) NE of Ipswich (TM 286637)*   Oval bailey with high curtain wall and open-backed square wall towers of *c.* 1190, 13th-century great hall converted to Poor House. Outer earthwork baileys to north and south. (EH)

33 Goodrich, *Herefordshire, 8 km (5 miles) SW of Ross-on-Wye (SO 577200)*   Square keep of mid 12th century, incorporated in rectangular castle of late 13th century with round corner towers, massive gatehouse and barbican. Domestic buildings ranged round central courtyard. Outer curtain with round corner towers on two sides. (EH)

34 Guildford, *Surrey (SU 997494)* Motte, with traces of bailey. Remains of polygonal shell keep on motte. Square keep of three storeys built on side of motte.

35 Hadleigh, *Essex, 6·4 km (4 miles) W of Southend (TQ 810860)* Irregular octagonal enclosure with curtain wall and D-plan wall towers of 13th century. East side rebuilt with two massive towers in 14th century, and barbican added. Foundations of two successive halls. Much ruined by subsidence. (EH)

36 Castle Hedingham, *Essex, 14·4 km (9 miles) N of Braintree (TL 787359)* Ringwork and bailey. Square keep of five storeys in centre of ringwork, with remains of forebuilding.

37 Helmsley, *N Yorkshire, 43·4 km (27 miles) W of Scarborough (SE 611837)* Rectangular enclosure with double rampart and ditch. Curtain with round wall towers and two gatehouses of *c.* 1200. D-plan keep of same date, altered in early 14th century. Elaborate south barbican and simpler north barbican of mid 13th century. Foundations of domestic buildings of 14th–15th centuries. (EH)

38 Kenilworth, *Warwickshire, 9·6 km (6 miles) SW of Coventry (SP 279723)* Large oval outer bailey with curtain, wall towers and gatehouse of early 13th century, connected by earth dam to barbican and protected by lake: new gatehouse built in 16th century. Inner bailey with square keep of two storeys: domestic buildings of mid 14th century. Many alterations of 16th century. (EH)

39 Kilpeck, *Herefordshire, 14·4 km (9 miles) SW of Hereford (SO 444305)* Motte with three baileys and village enclosure. Remains of shell keep on motte. Chapel of 12th century in town enclosure.

40 Kirby Muxloe, *Leicestershire, 8 km (5 miles) W of Leicester (SK 524046)* Rectangular moated castle of later 15th century, left unfinished in 1483. Original intention was to build four ranges of brick buildings round rectangular courtyard, with square corner towers and great gatehouse. Only lower part of gatehouse and one corner tower survives. (EH)

41 Lancaster, *Lancashire (SD 473619)*   Square keep of two storeys (later heightened), possibly of late 11th or early 12th century. Part of bailey curtain survives, with one round and two square wall towers. Massive gatehouse of 15th century. Castle extensively rebuilt as prison in 1800.

42 Launceston, *Cornwall (SX 331847)*   Tall motte with irregular bailey. Round keep of two storeys of early 13th century within earlier shell keep on motte, with lower outer shell wall, approached by defended stair. South gatehouse of 12th century and north gatehouse of 14th century. Bailey curtain of 12th century. (EH)

43 Lewes, *E Sussex (TQ 415101)*   Oval bailey with motte at each end. Shell keep with semi-octagonal wall towers on western motte: remains of another shell keep on eastern motte. Bailey curtain wall with remains of square gatehouse and square wall towers of early 12th century. Small barbican gatehouse of 14th century.

44 Lincoln, *Lincolnshire (SK 975718)*   Sub-rectangular enclosure in corner of defences of Roman town. Two mottes, one with polygonal shell keep and one with square tower built up within the mound. Curtain and square western gatehouse of late 11th or early 12th century: eastern gatehouse much altered. (Note also west end of cathedral, strongly built in the 1080s and used as siege castle in 1141, but subsequently altered.)

45 Longtown, *Herefordshire, 25·7 km (16 miles) SW of Hereford (SO 321292)*   Motte with large sub-rectangular bailey divided into two parts, within earthworks of Roman fort. Curtain and square gatehouse of late 12th century. Round keep of three storeys, with small semicircular buttresses, on motte. (EH)

46 Ludlow, *Salop (SO 508746)*   Curtain, large square gatehouse and four square wall towers, all of late 11th century. Gateway blocked, and gatehouse heightened and converted to keep. Outer bailey with curtain added in later 12th century. Circular chapel of early 12th century and domestic buildings of 13th and 14th centuries in inner bailey.

47 Maxstoke. *Warwickshire, 12·8 km (8 miles) E of Birmingham (SP 234866)*   Rectangular moated enclosure of mid 14th century, with curtain, octagonal corner towers and tall gatehouse.

162

48 Middleham, *N Yorkshire, 29 km (18 miles) NW of Ripon (SE 128887)* (i) Motte and bailey. (ii) Nearby, a large rect-angular keep of two storeys, built *c.* 1170, within later quad-rangular castle of 13th century, much rebuilt in 14th and 15th centuries. Gatehouse of early 14th century. Outer bailey obli-terated (EH)

49 Neroche, *Somerset, 11·2 km (7 miles) S of Taunton (ST 271158)* Large low motte added in late 11th century to sub-rectangular earthwork enclosure, built soon after Conquest and set within larger outer enclosure of uncertain date. Foundations of a tower and curtain wall found by excavation on motte.

50 Newark-on-Trent, *Nottinghamshire (SK 796541)* Quadri-lateral enclosure with rectangular corner tower and gate-house of three storeys, all of 12th century (eastern half of enclosure destroyed). Curtain with polygonal corner turret and wall tower of 13th century. Remains of 12th-century crypt below site of later hall.

51 New Buckenham, *Norfolk, 24 km (15 miles) SW of Norwich (TL 084904)* Ringwork with horseshoe bailey and square village enclosure. Round keep (badly damaged) at one side of ringwork has been partly buried when rampart was heightened.

52 Newcastle-upon-Tyne, *Tyne and Wear (NZ 253639)* Triangular enclosure much damaged by railway in 19th century. Part of the late 12th-century curtain survives, with square keep of three storeys. Large square gatehouse with oval barbican tower of mid 13th century, and postern gate of 12th century.

53 Norham, *Northumberland, 9·6 km (6 miles) SW of Berwick-upon-Tweed (NT 906474)* Oval ringwork with crescentic bailey. Square keep of three storeys built c. 1160 and altered in 15th century: gatehouse and curtain of same date, latter rebuilt in 16th century. Bailey gatehouse enlarged in 15th cen-tury and 12th-century curtain rebuilt in 13th century. (EH)

54 Norwich, *Norfolk (TG 232085)* Small low motte extended in early 12th century to carry large lavishly decorated hall-keep of two storeys (now a museum). Baileys obliterated.

55 Nunney, *Somerset, 8 km (5 miles) SW of Frome (ST 737457)* Outer bailey destroyed. Tall keep or tower house of

163

four storeys built in French style in late 14th century: rectangular plan with large round corner turrets. Moat. (EH)

56 Odiham, *Hampshire, 12·8 km (8 miles) E of Basingstoke (SU 726519)* Two rectangular baileys formerly surrounded by earthworks and a moat: small outer enclosure, also moated. Octagonal keep of three storeys, with pilaster buttresses at corners, built 1207–10.

57 Old Sarum, *Wiltshire, 4·8 km (3 miles) N of Salisbury (SU138327)* Outer bailey formed by earthworks of prehistoric hill fort. Ringwork of late 11th century, with remains of curtain and internal buildings of early and later 12th century. Foundations of 11th-century cathedral in outer bailey. (EH)

58 Orford, *Suffolk, 32 km (20 miles) E of Ipswich (TM 419499)* Bailey with curtain and open-backed square wall towers destroyed, surviving only as earthworks. Polygonal keep of three storeys with forebuilding and three large projecting rectangular turrets. (EH)

59 Pevensey, *E Sussex, 8 km (5 miles) NE of Eastbourne (TQ 644048)* Sub-rectangular enclosure of 11th century, set in corner of large oval Roman fort with curtain and wall towers of 3rd century. Curtain, gatehouse and D-plan wall towers of early 13th century. Hall of late 11th century converted to keep with projecting buttresses in 12th century (now much damaged). (EH)

60 Peveril, *Derbyshire, 24 km (15 miles) SW of Sheffield (SK 150826)* Triangular bailey with curtain of late 11th and early 12th century. Square keep of two storeys added astride curtain c. 1176. Foundations of hall of early 13th century, and remains of earlier hall and chapel of later 11th or earlier 12th century. (EH)

61 Pleshey, *Essex, 12·8 km (8 miles) NW of Chelmsford (TL 666144)* Motte and bailey within large village enclosure. Bailey originally to north of motte (now marked by line of street), rebuilt in later 12th century to south of motte. Excavation has revealed the foundations of a chapel in the southern bailey and of a brick keep on the motte.

62 Pontefract, *W Yorkshire (SE 460224)* Oval inner bailey, with rectangular outer bailey divided into two parts, with

164

curtain, square gatehouses and barbican. Inner bailey with curtain and D-plan wall towers of late 12th or early 13th century. Quadrifoil keep of mid 13th century on plinth of revetted rock.

63 Portchester, *Hampshire (SU 625046)* Outer bailey formed by Roman fort, with curtain and D-plan wall towers of 3rd century (gatehouses rebuilt in 12th century and again in 14th century). Inner bailey with keep of two storeys (later heightened), curtain, square corner tower and square gatehouse (with later barbican), all of early 12th century: domestic buildings of 14th century. Church in outer bailey is all that survives of early 12th-century priory. (EH)

64 Restormel, *Cornwall, 1·6 km (1 mile) N of Lostwithiel (SX 104614)* Circular ringwork with square stone gatehouse and single wall tower or small keep, all of late 11th century. Converted to shell keep in 12th century: internal buildings rebuilt against shell wall and projecting wall tower converted to chapel in 13th century. (EH)

65 Richard's Castle, *Herefordshire, 6·4 km (4 miles) S of Ludlow (SO 483703)* Tall motte with crescentic bailey. Remains of octagonal keep of 12th century, with projecting chapel, on motte. Foundations of early 13th-century curtain with D-plan towers, and square gatehouse of 12th century.

66 Richmond, *N Yorkshire, 19·3 km (12 miles) SW of Darlington (NZ 173007)* Large triangular bailey with curtain, square wall towers, hall and large square gatehouse of late 11th century. Gatehouse blocked, heightened and converted to keep in 12th century, when barbican added. One of the wall towers contains the chapel. (EH)

67 Castle Rising, *Norfolk, 6·4 km (4 miles) NE of King's Lynn (TF 666246)* Large oval ringwork built across earlier rectangular earthwork, which serves as bailey. Square gatehouse of 12th century leads into ringwork with large hall-keep of *c.* 1140: keep heightened, or upper part rebuilt, *c.* 1200. (EH)

68 Rochester, *Kent (TQ 742686)* Oval enclosure with curtain wall of late 11th century and square wall towers rebuilt in 14th century. Square keep of four storeys with forebuilding, built 1127–40. (Note also remains of motte and bailey to south, and Gandulf's Tower at north side of cathedral). (EH)

69 Rockingham, *Northamptonshire, 1·6 km (1 mile) N of Corby (SP 867914)* Motte (modified for artillery in 17th century) with two quadrilateral baileys. Gatehouse, and part of curtain, of later 13th century: remainder of curtain rebuilt in 16th century. Hall of 13th century incorporated in 16th-century house. Castle much altered in 19th century.

70 Sandal, *W Yorkshire (SE 337182)* Large motte with circular bailey. Remains of large round keep of 13th century with massive projecting towers on motte, with defended stair approached from a round barbican. Much ruined.

71 St Briavels, *Gloucestershire, 19·3 km (12 miles) SE of Monmouth (SO 558046)* Ringwork with curtain, remains of domestic buildings and fragments of square keep, all of later 12th century. Large gatehouse and chapel of late 13th century.

72 Scarborough, *N Yorkshire (TA 048892)* Huge outer bailey formed by natural headland, with remains of Roman signal station. Small inner bailey with curtain of 12th century and square keep (much damaged) commanding narrow approach to headland: elaborate barbican. Remains of two separate halls in outer bailey. (EH)

73 Sherborne Old Castle, *Dorset (ST 648168)* Rectangular bailey with angles chamfered off. Curtain wall of early 12th century with three square gatehouses and large outer enclosure or barbican with defended gate passage. Small keep with four ranges of domestic buildings of early 12th century grouped round courtyard in middle of bailey. Foundations of later domestic buildings. (EH)

74 Sulgrave, *Northamptonshire, 12·8 km (8 miles) NE of Banbury (SP 556454)* Ringwork with at least one bailey (now obliterated) on site of earlier Saxon manor house. Excavation has revealed the foundations of a hall and chamber built soon after the Conquest. Abandoned early in the 12th century.

75 Tamworth, *Staffordshire (SK 206038)* Medium sized motte with bailey (now obliterated). Polygonal shell keep, with square wall tower near entrance acting as a small keep. Later interior buildings may echo medieval arrangements.

76 Tattershall, *Lincolnshire, 19·3 km (12 miles) NW of Boston (TF 210575)* Quadrangular moated castle, originally with curtain, D-plan wall towers and gatehouse of 13th century. Rebuilt in mid 15th century, with large machicolated tower house acting as an independent chamber block adjoining the hall. Only the tower house now survives. (NT)

77 Thetford, *Norfolk (TL 875828)*   Huge motte 20 m (*c.* 65 ft) high. Bailey converted from prehistoric hill fort, with two lines of rampart and ditch surviving at north side only.

78 Tickhill, *S Yorkshire, 11·2 km (7 miles) E of Rotherham (SK 593928)*   Motte and bailey, with counterscarp bank to north and east. Foundations of polygonal shell keep on motte, with pilaster buttresses at angles. Curtain with square gatehouse of late 11th or early 12th century.

79 Totnes, *Devon (SX 800605)*   Tall motte with oval bailey. Excavation revealed stone foundation for a timber tower carried up through body of motte. Shell keep with mural stairs and latrine on motte, rebuilt in 14th century. Bailey curtain of 12th century also rebuilt at same time. (EH)

80 Tower of London *(TQ 336805)*   Finest of all hall-keeps, *c.* 1080s, originally of three storeys (top floor added later).   Octagonal wall tower, short length of curtain and gate of *c.* 1200. Main inner curtain with D-plan wall towers of second half of 13th century: one massive round tower on line of curtain served as royal chamber. Outer curtain, barbican and moat added in 1270s. Numerous later alterations and additions, especially in 19th century. (DOE)

81 Trematon, *Cornwall, 9·6 km (6 miles) NW of Plymouth (SX 410580)*   Tall motte with irregular oval bailey. Crenellated shell keep and bailey curtain of 12th century. Square gatehouse of same date, later rebuilt.

82 Warkworth, *Northumberland, 12·8 km (8 miles) SE of Alnwick (NU 247058)*   Motte with rectangular bailey. Curtain and wall towers mainly of early 13th century. Gatehouse of same date, with later machicolation. Hall and domestic buildings mainly of 14th century. Large unfinished chapel of mid 15th century. Cruciform tower house of late 14th century on motte. (EH)

83 Warwick, *Warwickshire (SP 283647)*   Tall motte with sub-rectangular bailey. Remains of octagonal shell keep on motte. Curtain wall of 12th century. East front rebuilt in 1380s with two massive corner towers, tall gatehouse and barbican: domestic buildings rebuilt at same time. Remains of large rectangular keep of 1480s.

84 Windsor, *Berkshire (SU 970770)*   Tall motte with two baileys. Shell keep (doubled in height in early 19th century) with 14th-century internal buildings. Curtain and square wall towers of 1170s round upper bailey. 13th-century curtain with D-plan wall towers round lower bailey. St George's Chapel, late 15th-century. Many alterations and additions, especially during early 19th century.

85 York, *N Yorkshire (SE 606515 and 603513)*   Two motte and bailey castles on opposite sides of river. Bailey of southern castle obliterated. Northern castle has quatrifoil keep of two storeys on motte, built 1245–59: bailey partly obscured by later buildings. (EH)

WALES

86 Beaumaris, *Anglesey, 8 km (5 miles) NE of Menai bridge (SH 328707)*   Concentric castle of 1295–1300, left unfinished. Square inner bailey with curtain, round corner towers, D-plan intermediary wall towers and two great gatehouses (only half built). Octagonal outer curtain with small round wall towers. Moat with defended dock for ships. (C)

87 Bronllys, *Powys, 12·8 km (8 miles) NE of Brecon (SO 149348)*   Motte and bailey. Round keep of three storeys of *c.* 1176 on motte. (C, keep only).

88 Caernarvon, *Gwynedd (SH 477626)*   Palatial castle begun in 1283 and left unfinished in 1330. Plan conforms to that of earlier motte and bailey on same site. High curtain wall with firing galleries and octagonal wall towers, one capped with three turrets and serving as keep. Two gatehouses, both incomplete but immensely strong. Foundations of hall and domestic buildings. Fortified town attached, with curtain and open-backed D-plan wall towers. (C)

89 Caerphilly, *Glamorgan (ST 155871)*   Concentric castle begun in 1271, surrounded by artificial lake. Quadrangular inner bailey with curtain, large round corner towers, huge D-plan kitchen tower and two gatehouses. Low outer curtain with two smaller open-backed gatehouses. Outer bailey or 'hornwork' to west. Fortified dam to east, acting as barbican, with massive square buttresses and octagonal wall towers. Earthworks of earlier castle of 1268 nearby to north-east. (C)

168

90 Cardiff, *Glamorgan (ST180767)* Motte with square bailey on line of Roman fort, the south and east walls of which were rebuilt to form bailey curtain. Polygonal shell keep of 12th century on motte. Castle much altered in 19th century.

91 Carew, *Dyfed, 6·4 km (4 miles) NW of Pembroke (SN 045037)* Quadrangular castle with small outer bailey. Gatehouse of *c.* 1200, later blocked. Curtain, hall, D-plan wall tower and semi-octagonal chapel tower of late 13th century. Great hall with square corner towers of *c.* 1300. Outer gate and many internal alterations of *c.* 1500. North front completely rebuilt 1588–92.

92 Carreg Cennen, *Dyfed, 4·8 km (3 miles) SE of Llandeilo (SN668190)* Square inner bailey of late 13th century: curtain with round, square and octagonal wall towers, and gatehouse approached by long defended stair ramp forming a barbican. Rectangular outer bailey of early 14th century, with remains of curtain with small round turrets. (C)

93 Castell Y Bere, *Gwynedd, 14·4 km (9 miles) NE of Towyn (SH 667086)* Irregular elongated enclosure with curtain, square keep-like tower, round wall tower, and two large D-plan towers at opposite ends of the enclosure, all of 13th century. Square gatehouse protected by barbican with two small square towers. Much ruined. (C)

94 Castell Coch, *Glamorgan, 8 km (5 miles) NE of Cardiff (ST 131826)* Late 13th-century castle, much ruined: completely rebuilt in 1875. Oval bailey with curtain, three large wall towers and square gatehouse. Domestic buildings with wooden galleries, etc., decorated in late Victorian Neo-Gothic style. Details of reconstruction not always correct, but castle gives a good overall impression of what a small 13th-century castle might have looked like. (C)

95 Chepstow, *Gwent (ST 533941)* Irregular inner bailey with first-floor hall (heightened in 13th century) and remains of curtain of late 11th century: curtain rebuilt in late 12th century, 13th century and again in 17th century. North barbican, and outer bailey to south with gatehouse, of mid 13th century: large wall tower of *c.* 1270 serving as independent chamber block to domestic range with two halls. Note also walls, with D-plan towers, of adjoining fortified town. (C)

96 Chirk, *Clwyd, 11·2 km (7 miles) NW of Oswestry (SJ 281377)* Built *c.* 1289–95. Quadrangular castle with large round corner towers and D-plan intermediary wall towers. South front altered in 16th century and rebuilt in 17th century. Internal buildings much altered and rebuilt in 18th and 19th centuries.

97 Cilgerran, *Dyfed, 3·2 km (2 miles) SE of Cardigan (SN 195431)* Polygonal inner bailey with curtain, two large wall towers of four storeys and square gatehouse, all of early 13th century: curtain at west and north sides rebuilt in later 13th century. Foundations of domestic buildings. Triangular outer bailey with fragment of curtain wall of late 13th century. (C)

98 Coity, *Glamorgan, 3·2 km (2 miles) N of Bridgend (SS 923816)* Ringwork, with later rectangular bailey with square wall towers. Polygonal curtain, gatehouse and square keep, all of 12th century: oval latrine tower of 13th century. Hall, chapel and other domestic buildings of 14th century. (C)

99 Conway, *Gwynedd (SH 784774)* Built 1283–7. Square inner bailey with curtain and massive round corner towers capped by stair turrets: royal apartments of two storeys. Rectangular outer bailey with round wall towers and corner towers: great hall and foundations of service buildings. East and west barbicans with open-backed round towers. Note attached fortified town, with curtain and open-backed D-plan wall towers. (C). Earlier castle of Degannwy, 3·2 km (2 miles) to N.

100 Criccieth, *Gwynedd (SH 500377)* Outer bailey formed by Welsh castle of early 13th century with three rectangular towers, now largely obliterated. Lozenge-shaped inner bailey built 1285–92, with great gatehouse and remains of polygonal curtain without wall towers. (C)

101 Degannwy, *Gwynedd, 3·2 km (2 miles) N of Conway (SH 781794)* Predecessor of Conway Castle, built in 1244–54 on site fortified since at least 9th century: slighted in 1263. Irregular oval bailey with traces of curtain and gatehouse, between two small hillocks forming natural mottes. Excavation has revealed that east hillock was formerly defended by large open-backed D-plan tower: West hillock formed inner bailey with curtain, hall and large round tower. Castle reoccupied during campaign of 1277, replaced by Conway in 1283.

102 Denbigh, *Clwyd (SJ059660)* Built in 1282 in corner of fortified town of same date. Town walls built first, forming south and west sides of castle, with D-plan wall towers. Castle completed *c.* 1285 by building thicker curtain with octagonal wall towers to enclose polygonal bailey: huge gatehouse of three interlinked octagonal towers. Low outer curtain and barbican added 1295. Foundations of domestic buildings. (C)

103 Dolbadarn, *Gwynedd, 12·8 km (8 miles) S of Bangor (SH 586598)* Irregular triangular bailey with foundations of curtain and two rectangular wall towers. Round keep of three storeys of early 13th century, with projecting latrine turret. Foundations of hall. (C)

104 Dolwyddelan, *Gwynedd, 9·6 km (6 miles) SW of Betws-y-Coed (SH722523)* Polygonal bailey with foundations of curtain wall of early 13th century. Small rectangular keep of two storeys (top floor added in 15th century, battlements modern). Remains of second rectangular tower of 1280s. (C)

105 Dynevor, *Dyfed, 1·6 km (1 mile) W of Llandeilo (SN 611217)* Polygonal enclosure with rock-cut ditch. Curtain of 12th century with round corner tower, square corner turret and latrine tower, survives at south and west sides only: rest of curtain rebuilt in 15th century. Round keep of early 13th century (top part modern). Hall rebuilt in 15th century.

106 Ewloe, *Clwyd, 19·3 km (12 miles) W of Chester (SJ 288675)* Triangular inner bailey with curtain and D-plan keep of two storeys of early 13th century, raised above level of irregular outer bailey with curtain and round corner tower of two storeys, also of early-mid 13th-century date. (C)

107 Flint, *Clwyd (SJ 247733)* Built 1277–86. Square inner bailey with curtain and three round corner towers: unusually designed round keep of three storeys occupies fourth corner of bailey, standing within its own moat (now dry). Rectangular outer bailey, lately destroyed. (C)

108 Grosmont, *Gwent, 22·5 km (14 miles) SW of Hereford (SO 405244)* Large low motte with traces of earthwork barbican. First-floor hall of 12th century: curtain with D-plan wall

171

towers and gatehouse of early 13th century. Gatehouse extended, and new domestic buildings added *c*.1330. (C)

109 Harlech, *Gwynedd (SH 581313)* Built 1283–9. Concentric castle with rectangular inner bailey with curtain, large round corner towers and gatehouse keep. Low outer curtain with small open-backed turrets. Foundations of domestic buildings in inner bailey. Former outer bailey to north, now largely destroyed. (C)

110 Haverfordwest, *Dyfed (SM 953157)* Polygonal bailey of 14th century, with curtain and square, open-backed and D-plan wall towers. Remains of large irregular outer bailey with curtain and square wall tower. Much altered and partly occupied by modern buildings.

111 Hawarden, *Clwyd, 11·2 km (7 miles) W of Chester (SJ 319653)* Motte and bailey, with complex outworks, possibly of prehistoric date. Round keep of two storeys of early 13th century on motte: polygonal bailey, with curtain with single solid D-plan tower and elaborate barbican. Foundations of domestic buildings of uncertain date.

112 Hen Domen, *Powys, 3·2 km (2 miles) NW of Montgomery (SO 214980)* Motte and bailey, with double rampart and ditch. Excavation has revealed the supports of a bridge leading to the motte and many wooden buildings in the bailey.

113 Kidwelly, *Dyfed, 12·8 km (8 miles) NW of Llanelli (SN 409071).* Semicircular ringwork of 12th century, rebuilt in late 13th century. Square inner bailey with curtain and tall round curtain towers of 1275. Hall and projecting chapel tower of 1280–1300. Outer bailey (on line of earlier ringwork) with curtain and open-backed D-plan towers of early 14th century. Gatehouse rebuilt in late 14th century. (C)

114 Laugharne, *Dyfed (SN 302107)* Small polygonal inner bailey, with two round wall towers of late 13th century, one (of four storeys) possibly serving as keep. Much altered in early 16th century when curtain rebuilt, new gatehouse constructed and domestic range added at south side (now destroyed). Outer bailey vanished.

115 Llanstephan, *Dyfed, 12·8 km (8 miles) SW of Carmarthen (SN 351101)* Ringwork and bailey of 12th century. Ringwork has remains of curtain of late 12th century (heightened

172

in early 13th century) with square gatehouse of early 13th century. Bailey with curtain, D-plan wall towers and gatehouse of later 13th century; gatehouse blocked and new gatehouse built alongside in late 15th century. (C)

116 Manorbier, *Dyfed, 9·6 km (6 miles) SW of Tenby (SS 064978)* Irregular inner bailey with polygonal curtain of *c.* 1230 with round curtain towers, enclosing small square tower and first-floor hall of 12th century. Chapel added *c.* 1260. Curtain heightened and gatehouse added in late 13th century. Extra accommodation added between hall and chapel, with projecting latrine wing, *c.* 1300. Outer bailey destroyed.

117 Monmouth, *Gwent (SO 507129)* Oval ringwork with sub-rectangular town enclosure, both much altered. Keep-like first-floor hall of late 11th century, with additions of 14th century. Great hall nearby, of late 13th century. Round tower or keep demolished when castle slighted in 1647 and house built 1673. (C)

118 Montgomery, *Powys (SO 221967)* Built 1224 to succeed Hen Domen (No. 112). Irregular oval inner bailey with curtain, great gatehouse and two D-plan wall towers (one rebuilt in later 13th century). Sub-rectangular outer bailey with curtain of mid 13th century. Much ruined. (C)

119 Ogmore, *Glamorgan, 4·8 km (3 miles) SW of Bridgend (SS 882769)* Oval ringwork with sub-rectangular bailey. Polygonal curtain of early 13th century enclosing small rectangular keep or first-floor hall of two storeys (later heightened) and chamber, both of 12th century. Hall of early 13th century. Bailey contains 14th-century court house and a lime-kiln of 13th century. (C)

120 Pembroke, *Dyfed (SM 982016)* Triangular inner bailey of *c.* 1200 with curtain, domed round keep of four storeys and hall; gate and south part of curtain destroyed. Outer bailey of early 13th century with curtain, round wall towers, gatehouse and a second hall. (C)

121 Raglan, *Gwent, 16 km (10 miles) SW of Monmouth (SO 415083)* Built 1461–9 on site of earlier motte and bailey. Hexagonal keep of four (originally five) storeys surrounded by low curtain with small turrets and moat. Within bailey, two courtyards separated by central block of buildings containing hall, chamber and chapel, and protected by curtain with machicolated hexagonal wall towers. Extensive domestic buildings of two storeys. (C)

122   Rhuddlan, *Clwyd, 4·8 km (3 miles) SE of Rhyl (SJ 026777)*   Built 1277–8. Concentric castle: lozenge-shaped inner bailey with two gatehouses and two round corner towers. Low outer curtain with massive buttresses and square turrets, fronted by moat. Defended dock at river edge. Note adjoining defended town and earlier motte and bailey to south. (C)

123   Skenfrith, *Powys, 17·7 km (11 miles) SW of Ross-on-Wye (SO 457202)*   Rectangular enclosure with curtain, round corner towers and round keep of three storeys, all of early 13th century, formerly surrounded by moat: D-plan wall tower added to one side in late 13th century. Gatehouse destroyed. Basements of domestic range of early 13th century (C)

124   Tretower, *Powys, 17·2 km (11 miles) SE of Brecon (SO 184214)*   (i) Low stone-revetted motte with 12th-century shell keep containing first floor hall and chamber, and 13th-century round keep: bailey with curtain and round corner towers (now a farmyard). (ii) Quadrangular manor house of 14th and 15th centuries, with two ranges of two-storey buildings, flanking courtyard with curtain wall. (C)

125   White Castle, *Gwent, 8 km (5 miles) E of Abergavenny (SO 380168)*   Large low motte with crescentic bailey and village enclosure. Motte has curtain of 12th century with foundations of small square keep. In 13th century castle was 'turned round': old gate blocked, new gatehouse built at opposite side of motte, and D-plan wall towers added to curtain: at same time, bailey provided with curtain wall, open-backed D-plan towers and gatehouse. (C)

SCOTLAND

126   Borthwick, *Lothian, 19·3 km (12 miles) SE of Edinburgh (NT 370597)*   Irregular bailey with curtain (with gun ports) and small square gatehouse of c. 1500. Machicolated tower house of five storeys of c. 1430, with two wings giving a U-plan.

127   Bothwell, *Strathclyde, 12·8 km (8 miles) SE of Glasgow (NS 688593)*   Remains of large round keep of three storeys, with fragment of curtain and round wall tower, all of late 13th century. Rectangular bailey with round and square wall towers of late 14th or early 15th century, and great hall of early 15th century. Traces of unfinished outer bailey with round wall towers and great gatehouse of late 13th century. (SDD)

128 Caerlaverock, *Dumfries and Galloway, 11·2 km (7 miles) SE of Dumfries (NY 026656)* Triangular bailey of late 13th century with curtain and two round machicolated corner towers, within moat: massive machicolated gatehouse occupies third corner of bailey. Hall-range of 16th century and other domestic buildings of 17th century. (SDD)

129 Claypotts, *Tayside, 4·8 km (3 miles) E of Dundee (NO 453318)* Rectangular tower house of four storeys of 1569–88, with two round corner towers offset to give a Z-plan. Corner towers have square chambers corbelled-out over the tops. (SDD)

130 Craigmillar, *Lothian, in SE outskirts of Edinburgh (NT 285710)* Rectangular tower house of four storeys of late 14th century, with single wing giving L-plan, within rectangular bailey with machicolated curtain and round corner towers (with gun ports) of 1427. Domestic buildings and irregular outer bailey of 16th century. (SDD)

131 Cubbie Roo's Castle (Cobbie Row), *Isle of Wyre, Orkney (HY 442264)* Remains of small square tower of mid 12th century within ringwork beside 12th-century chapel. Traces of adjoining buildings of later but uncertain age. (SDD)

132 Dirleton, *Lothian, 3·2 km (2 miles) SW of North Berwick (NT 516839)* Polygonal bailey with curtain and round wall towers of late 13th century. Curtain rebuilt in 14th century with square machicolated gatehouse and first-floor hall and chamber: chapel added in 15th century. Gatehouse and adjoining wall tower remodelled to form composite tower house in 16th century. (SDD)

133 Doune, *Central, 6·4 km (4 miles) W of Dunblane (NN 731011)* Built in later 14th century. Tall gatehouse of four storeys adjoining first-floor hall, the two forming frontal screen to rectangular bailey with curtain and projecting kitchen tower: other domestic buildings left unfinished.

134 Doune of Invernochty, *Grampian, 16 km (10 miles) N of Ballater (NJ 351129)* Huge oval motte with counterscarp bank: ditch flooded from pond controlled by large earth dam.

Remains of shell keep or curtain enclosing foundations of tower and chapel.

135 Drum, *Grampian, 16 km (10 miles) SW of Aberdeen (NJ 796005)* Simple rectangular tower house of five storeys of early or mid 14th century, with crenellated parapet. Mansion of 17th century attached.

136 Duffus, *Grampian, 6·4 km (4 miles) N of Elgin (NJ 189673)* Motte and bailey. Rectangular keep of three storeys of later 14th century on motte: plain polygonal curtain of same date round bailey. North side of bailey rebuilt in later 15th century, with domestic range. Larger outer precinct earthwork. (SDD)

137 Dunstaffnage, *Strathclyde, 4·8 km (3 miles) NE of Oban (NM 883345)* Quadrangular castle of mid 13th century set on scarped boss of rock. Curtain with two corner towers, one (of three storeys) serving as keep. Tower house of 17th century built over 13th-century entrance. (SDD)

138 Edinburgh, *Lothian (NT 251735)* Irregular enclosure with buildings of many periods, on site fortified since at least 6th century. Chapel of 12th century. Remains of tower house of 1367–79 (encased in 16th-century gun bastion). Gatehouse and palace buildings of early 16th century. Barracks and gun emplacements of 18th century. Many 19th-century alterations. (SDD)

139 Hermitage, *Borders, 8 km (5 miles) N of Newcastleton (NY 497961)* Remains of large quadrangular castle of earlier 14th century, incorporated in huge rectangular tower house of late 14th century with single wing giving an L-plan. Large machicolated square corner towers added, *c.* 1400. Original wing extended in early 15th century. (SDD)

140 Inverlochy, *Highland, 3·2 km (2 miles) NE of Fort William (NN 121755)* Square bailey of mid-late 13th century with curtain and round wall towers, one corner tower (of three storeys) being larger than the others and serving as keep. (SDD)

141 Kildrummy, *Grampian, 16 km (10 miles) W of Alford (NJ 455164)* (i) Motte and bailey. (ii) Nearby, to south-west, castle of mid 13th century with polygonal bailey enclosed by curtain with round and D-plan wall towers and great gatehouse of late 13th century. One wall tower larger than the others and

176

serving as keep (now destroyed). Foundations of domestic buildings and chapel. (SDD)

142 Kiessimul, *Isle of Barra,* Western Isles (NN 666979)   Built on small islet. Square keep of four storeys, with polygonal curtain wall. Date uncertain, but possibly of mid 13th century. Domestic buildings rebuilt in 18th century.

143 Loch Doon, *Strathclyde, 11·2 km (7 miles) S of Dalmellington (NX 484950)*   Originally built on island in loch: rebuilt on mainland by SDD. Polygonal curtain of late 13th or early 14th century: foundations of internal buildings of uncertain date. (SDD)

144 Mingary, *Highland, on SW coast of Ardnamurchan, 1·6 km (1 mile) SE of Kilchoan (NM 502631)*   High polygonal curtain, with small mural chambers, of 13th century: small turrets of 17th century and internal barrack block of 18th century.

145 Mousa, *Shetland, on Mousa Island (HU 457237)*   Round tower or *broch* of c. 1st century AD, with open central courtyard, mural chambers at ground level and mural passages above. (SDD)

146 Ravenscraig, *Fife, in northern outskirts of Kirkcaldy (NT 291925)*   Built 1460–63.   Promontory site with neck of promontory barred by curtain with two large D-plan towers for cannon, one (of four storeys) serving as tower house or keep. Curtain raised and provided with artillery platform early in 16th century. (SDD)

147 Rothesay, *Strathclyde, Isle of Bute (NS 088646)*   Circular curtain wall or shell keep of late 12th or early 13th century, with round wall towers added in early 13th century. Three-storeyed gatehouse, two-storeyed chapel of early 16th century. (SDD)

148 Skipness, *Strathclyde, 12·8 km (8 miles) SE of Tarbert (NR 909577)*   Rectangular three-storey hall-house and chapel of early 13th century, incorporated in later 13th-century quadrangular castle: tower house added in 16th century.

149 Stirling, *Central (NS 790940)*   Irregular enclosure with buildings mainly of 15th century and later, on site fortified for many centuries. Great hall of later 15th century, quadrangular palace buildings of early 16th century and chapel of late 16th century. Outer artillery defences, and many internal alterations, of 18th century. (SDD)

150 Sween, *Strathclyde, 25·7 km (16 miles) SW of Lochgilphead (NR 714788)* Rectangular enclosure, or lower part of keep, of later 12th century: foundations of 13th-century tower of two storeys at one corner and round tower of 16th century at the other. (SDD)

151 Tantallon, *Lothian, 4·8 km (3 miles) E of North Berwick. (NT 596850)* Promontory site, with extremely high curtain or screen wall with round corner towers and gatehouse of four storeys across neck of promontory. Foundations of domestic buildings. (SDD)

152 Threave, *Dumfries and Galloway, 3·2 km (2 miles) W of Castle Douglas (NX 739623)* Rectangular tower house of five storeys of late 14th century, within rectangular bailey with curtain, gatehouse and round corner towers (with gun ports) of mid 15th century. (SDD)

153 Tioram, *Highland, on tidal islet off south shore of Loch Moidart (NM 661725)* Polygonal bailey of 13th century, with curtain and square keep of four storeys, on boss of rock. Tower house and domestic buildings of 16th century.

ISLE OF MAN

154 Rushen, *near Castleton (SC 265675)* Square keep of two storeys of later 12th century, with square projecting mid-wall turrets of *c.* 1200: keep heightened and gatehouse added to north side in early 14th century. Polygonal curtain with square corner turrets, outer gatehouse and barbican of later 14th century: keep and inner gatehouse heightened at same time. Round gun tower, outer barbican and surrounding glacis of 16th century.

NORTHERN IRELAND

155 Ardglass, *Down (J 561372)* (i) Ardglass Castle: two-storey range of 15th century (west part incorporated into house of 18th century), with small square towers projecting to north. (ii) Cowd Castle: small square tower house of two storeys of late 15th or early 16th century. (iii) Margaret's Castle: square tower house of three storeys of 15th century, with two wings giving a U-plan. (iv) Jordan's Castle: square tower house of four storeys of 15th century, with two wings giving a U-plan.

156 Carrickfergus, *Antrim (J 414873)* Inner bailey of late

12th century, with curtain and square keep of four storeys of c. 1200. Middle bailey with foundations of curtain and square wall tower of early 13th century. Outer bailey with gatehouse of early-mid 13th century. Altered for artillery defence in 16th century and again in 19th century. (DOE)

157 Dromore, *Down (J 206532)* Motte and bailey of late 12th century. Tall motte (later heightened) with square bailey, both surrounded by outer rampart and ditch on north and east sides. (DOE)

158 Dundrum, *Down (J 404370)* Oval inner bailey with polygonal curtain of c. 1200, and round keep of three storeys of early 13th century: gatehouse of later 13th century. Outer bailey with curtain of late 13th century and house of 17th century. (DOE)

159 Dunluce, *Antrim, 6·4 km (4 miles) E of Portrush (D 905415)* Castle of 13th century, much altered in 17th century. Remains of curtain with two round wall towers of 13th century: gatehouse of c. 1600: large house of early 17th century and remains of other domestic buildings of same date. (DOE)

160 Greencastle, *Down, 9·6 km (6 miles) SW of Kilkeel (J 247118)* (i) Motte. (ii) Nearby, quadrilateral bailey with fragments of curtain and D-plan corner towers of 13th century. Rectangular keep of two storeys of c. 1260, heightened and much altered in late 15th and early 16th centuries, and single-storey building of uncertain use. Remains of 16th-century domestic buildings and modern farm. (DOE)

161 Kilclief, *Down, 4·8 km (3 miles) S of Strangford (J 202532)* Square tower house of four storeys of c. 1420, with two small wings giving a U-plan. (DOE)

162 Monea, *Fermanagh, 11·2 km (7 miles) NW of Enniskillen, (H 164494)* Rectangular tower house of three storeys of 1618, with two round corner towers capped by corbelled-out square chambers, and two small corbelled-out round corner turrets. Remains of rectangular bailey with two round corner towers. (DOE)

REPUBLIC OF IRELAND

163 Adare, *Limerick, 16 km (10 miles) SW of Limerick (R 460467)* Oval ringwork with square keep of three storeys of early 13th century, much damaged: curtain (later rebuilt) and square gatehouse. Sub-rectangular bailey with square gatehouse and first-floor hall of early 13th century; aisled hall of later 13th century nearby.

164 Athenry, *Galway, 22·5 km (14 miles) E of Galway (M 504280)* Bailey with polygonal curtain and round corner towers of 13th century, much ruined. Keep, or early tower house, of three storeys, of mid 13th century. (OPW)

165 Athlone, *West Meath (N 040415)* Motte and bailey: motte later revetted in stone. Polygonal curtain with round corner towers, and polygonal keep, of mid 13th century. Now much altered and used as barracks. (OPW)

166 Ballintober, *Roscommon, 16 km (10 miles) NW of Roscommon (M 726747)* Square bailey with curtain, polygonal corner towers and gatehouse of late 13th century. Possibly an Irish copy of Roscommon Castle (no. 187).

167 Ballymoon, *Carlow, 3·2 km (2 miles) E of Bagenalstown (S 739615)* Quadrangular castle of late 13th century or early 14th century. Square bailey with curtain and three square projecting turrets: traces of domestic buildings of two storeys over cellars on all sides of bailey. (OPW)

168 Ballymote, *Sligo, 22·5 km (14 miles) S of Sligo (G 661155)* Square bailey with curtain and round corner towers, and intermediary wall towers of square or D-plan, all of late 13th century: gatehouse destroyed.

169 Blarney, *Cork, 9·6 km (6 miles) NW of Cork (W 605753)* Rectangular tower house of four storeys of mid 15th century, adjoining earlier square tower which now forms wing to main block: machicolated parapets probably added at end of 15th century.

170 Bunratty, *Clare, 12·8 km (8 miles) NW of Limerick (R 450610)* Rectangular tower house of three storeys of late 15th century, with large square corner towers linked by machicolations across the short ends of the building. (OPW)

171 Burnchurch, *Kilkenny, 9·6 km (6 miles) S of Kilkenny (S 475473)* Rectangular tower house of four storeys of 15th century: gable walls carried up one storey higher than side walls as wide turrets with mural passages. (OPW)

172 Cahir, *Tipperary (S 050247)* Castle of 15th and 16th centuries. Bailey divided into two parts with curtain, wall towers (of square, round and polygonal plan), keep of three storeys and hall (now a church). (OPW)

173 Carlingford, *Louth (J189120)* Irregular D-plan bailey. West part with curtain, single square wall tower and remains of square gatehouse, all of early 13th century: east part rebuilt in mid 13th century as massive hall and chamber block of three storeys. (OPW)

174 Carrigogunnell, *Limerick, 9·6 km (6 miles) W of Limerick (R 497552)* Irregular oval bailey on high rock. Plain curtain of 15th century. Two towers, of three and four storeys, of late 15th or 16th century. Remains of other domestic buildings of uncertain date. Much ruined, having been slighted in 1691.

175 Castleroche, *Louth, 8 km (5 miles) NW of Dundalk (J 991119)* Irregular bailey with high plain curtain, single large D-plan tower or bastion and gatehouse, all of mid 13th century: hall of two storeys. Traces of outer bailey. (OPW)

176 Clara, *Kilkenny, 6·4 km (4 miles) E of Kilkenny (S 574578)* Rectangular tower house of five storeys of late 15th century, extremely well preserved. Small rectangular bailey or 'bawn' acting as forecourt. (OPW)

177 Dunamase, *Laoighis, 6·4 km (4 miles) W of Maryborough (S 530983)* Irregular oval inner bailey of mid 13th century with curtain, square gatehouse and remains of rectangular keep: triangular barbican and D-plan earthwork outer bailey. Slighted in 1650 and much ruined.

178 Dunsoghly, *Dublin, 9·6 km (6 miles) NW of Dublin (O 118432)* Square tower house of four storeys of 15th century with square corner towers rising above level of main block as turrets. Original roof of 15th century still survives. (OPW)

179 Ferns, *Wexford, 11·2 km (7 miles) NE of Enniscorthy (T 024500)* Large square keep of three storeys of early 13th century, with massive round corner towers (much damaged). No trace of bailey survives. (OPW)

180 Greencastle, *Donegal, 6·4 km (4 miles) NE of Moville (C 655404)* Irregular oval bailey with curtain and large gatehouse with octagonal towers, of early 14th century: square keep of at least two storeys. Slighted in 1555 and much ruined.

181   Lea, *Laoighis, 3·2 km (2 miles) E of Portarlington (N 573120)*   Oval inner bailey with remains of curtain and open-backed round wall towers: rectangular keep of three storeys of early 17th century, with massive round corner towers. Irregular outer bailey with curtain and gatehouse of late 13th century: gatehouse later blocked and new gate built alongside.

182   Limerick *(R 574572)*   Polygonal bailey with curtain, gatehouse and round corner towers of early 13th century (one tower replaced by artillery bastion in 1611). Corner towers lowered for artillery defence and vaulted to carry guns. Barracks of 18th century and modern buildings in bailey. (OPW)

183   Liscarroll, *Cork, 11·2 km (7 miles) NW of Buttevant (R 452124)*   Rectangular bailey with round corner towers, rect-angular gatehouse of three storeys, and small square mid wall tower on north side, all of 13th century. Traces of domestic buildings. (OPW)

184   Maynooth, *Kildare, 22·3 km (14 miles) W of Dublin (O 935375)*   Square keep of two storeys of early 13th century, much altered: square gatehouse of three storeys and fragment of curtain with postern turret and square wall tower. Domestic buildings rebuilt in 17th century. (OPW)

185   Nenagh, *Tipperary (R 865790)*   Round keep of four storeys of early 13th century (heightened *c.* 1860). Traces of small polygonal bailey with curtain and round corner towers, now almost entirely destroyed: gatehouse of early or mid 13th century, with later hall added at rear. (OPW)

186   Quin, *Clare, 9·6 km (6 miles) SE of Ennis (R 417745)*   Quadrangular castle of 1278–80 with curtain and round corner towers. Destroyed in 1288 and rebuilt as Francis-can friary in mid 15th century, with church and cloister. (OPW)

187   Roscommon, *(M 873652)*   Quadrangular castle of late 13th century with curtain, D-plan corner towers, massive gate-house of three storeys and square postern tower. Much altered for building of new domestic range in 1580, when large win-dows cut in curtain, gatehouse and corner towers. (OPW)

188   Roscrea, *Tipperary (S 130880)*   Polygonal bailey with curtain, two round corner towers and rectangular gatehouse of two storeys, all of late 13th century: gatehouse blocked and heightened in 17th century to form tower house. (OPW)

182

189 Swords, *Dublin 12·8 km (8 miles) N of Dublin (O 198473)*   Large polygonal bailey with curtain and three square wall towers (one serving as small keep) of 13th century. Gateway, with adjoining chapel with tower to east and domestic range to west. Foundations of chamber and hall. (OPW)

190 Trim, *Meath (N 805569)*   Motte and bailey of late 12th century. Triangular bailey with curtain and open-backed round wall towers of early 13th century: square gatehouse and round postern tower with barbican turret. Square keep of two storeys (later heightened) of *c.* 1200, with square towers projecting from wall faces. Remains of town wall. (OPW)

SITE LISTS

Note   Not every castle in the Gazetteer is indexed here: only the better preserved examples are listed. The numbers refer to the Gazetteer on pages 156-183 and to the maps on pages 186-189.

Ringworks   1, 30, 36, 51, 57, 64, 74, 98, 119, 163

Motte and Bailey Castles   10, 16, 20, 21, 29, 39, 42, 43, 44, 45, 49, 61, 65, 70, 75, 77, 79, 81, 84, 85, 87, 90, 112, 134, 136, 157, 165

Shell Keeps   4, 9, 16, 29, 31, 42, 43, 44, 64, 75, 79, 81, 84, 90, 124, 147

Fortified Halls and Hall-Keeps   1, 22, 54, 67, 80, 95, 117

Square Keeps   3, 6, 15, 17, 21, 24, 27, 33, 36, 38, 41, 48, 52, 53, 60, 63, 68, 72, 98, 104, 136, 142, 150, 154, 156, 160, 163, 164, 179, 180, 181, 184, 190

Round and Polygonal Keeps   18, 23, 42, 45, 51, 56, 58, 87, 103, 105, 107, 120, 121, 123, 124, 127, 141, 158, 165, 185

Gatehouses of 11th and 12th Centuries   4, 27, 30, 43, 46, 50, 64, 66, 73, 78

Gatehouses of 13th Century and later   6, 8, 11, 24, 27, 28, 37, 38, 41, 59, 69, 71, 80, 82, 83, 86, 88, 89, 95, 100, 109, 113, 128, 154, 156, 163, 166, 180, 182, 184, 187, 188, 190

Wall Towers (square) 16, 27, 30, 31, 32, 46, 66, 84, 173 (Round or D-Plan) 8, 11, 24, 27, 59, 63, 80, 84, 86, 88, 93, 96, 99, 109, 113, 127, 128, 132, 140, 141, 151, 166, 168, 182, 187, 190

Barbicans   23, 27, 33, 37, 43, 66, 70, 72, 80, 83, 89, 92, 99, 111, 154, 190

Edwardian Concentric Castles   33, 80, 86, 89, 109, 113, 122

Moated Castles   11, 14, 40, 55, 80, 86, 89, 128

Halls and Domestic Buildings   2, 11, 13, 20, 29, 46, 66, 73, 82, 83, 84, 98, 99, 108, 116, 121, 132, 133, 148, 149, 163, 173, 175

184

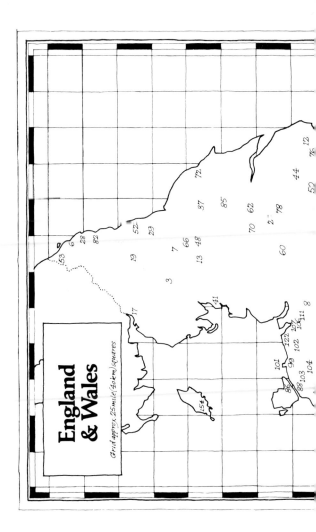

England
& Wales

Grid approx 25mile/40km squares

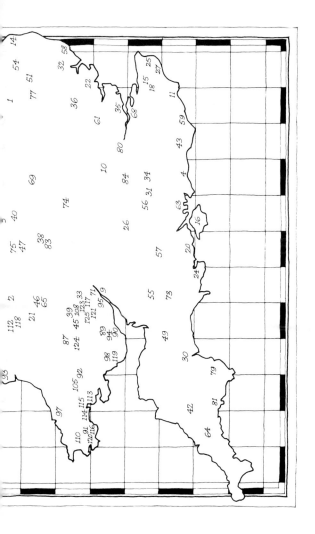

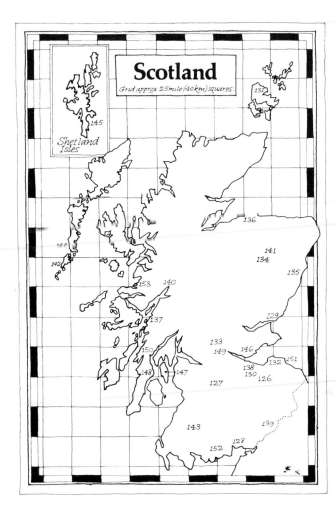

Scotland

Grid approx 2.5 mile (40km) squares.

131

145

Shetland Isles

142

136

141
134

135

153   140

129

137

133
149   146

150   138   132   151
                 130   126

148   147   127

143   139

152   128

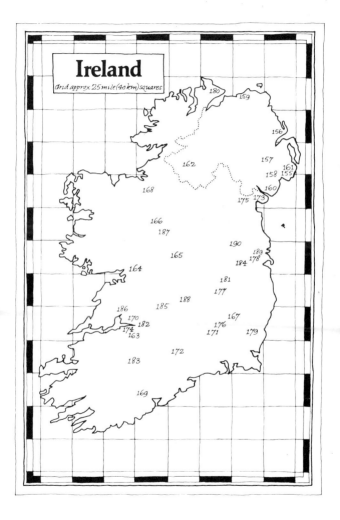

Ireland

Grid approx 25 mile (40 km) squares

180
159
156
157
161
155
158
162
160
175 173
168
166
187
190
189
165
184 178
164
181
177
186 185 188
170 182
176 167
174 163
171 179
172
183
169